ALSO BY NICHOLAS GAGE

Bones of Contention
The Bourlotas Fortune
Eleni

HELLAS

HELLAS

A PORTRAIT OF GREECE

By Nicholas Gage

VILLARD BOOKS

NEW YORK

1987

To the Memory of My Father
CHRISTOS GATZOYIANNIS

949.5
Gag

Portions of text were previously published in *Portrait of Greece*
by Nicholas Gage. Published by American Heritage Press, a subsidiary
of McGraw-Hill, Inc., in 1971.

The photos in this volume are used courtesy of:
Magnum Photos for Rene Burri;
Photo Researchers, Inc., for Margot Granitsas;
Michele Macrakis; and Reenie Schmerl.

Library of Congress Cataloging-in-Publication Data
Gage, Nicholas.
Hellas, a portrait of Greece.
Rev. ed. of: Portrait of Greece.   1971. 1. Greece.
2. Greece—Social life and customs—20th century.
I. Gage, Nicholas.   Portrait of Greece.
II. Title.
DF717.G25 1987   949.5   86-40120
ISBN 0-394-55694-1

Designed by Robert Bull

Manufactured in the United States of America
9   8   7   6   5   4   3   2
First edition

CONTENTS

153317

HELLAS

ONE

Land of Light

> "You should see the landscape of Greece.
> It would break your heart."
> LAWRENCE DURRELL,
> *Spirit of Place*

It all started with the land. The red, unpromising soil was sown with stones, but it brought forth the gods, the heroes, and the philosophers, the literature, the architecture, and the art. Jason's harvest of armed soldiers, grown in a day from dragon's teeth, seems no more miraculous. Yet when you walk among the stones of Greece and experience that combination of light and water and earth that is the Greek landscape, it all becomes inevitable. No other land could have produced such a people, and this land could have produced nothing else.

Islands make up one-fifth of the land area of Greece— over fourteen hundred of them, many as bare and gray as the shells of giant turtles floating on the water. The largely mountainous mainland is pocketed with small villages that hang precariously, as if about to spill into the valleys. Cypresses that look like candles and firs, myrtles, and fig trees grow on the mountainsides, and in the spring there are poppies like drops of blood and heather for the bees. Not much else can flourish here, except for the hardy mountain goats and, in the north, wild boar. The villagers gather the mountain herbs and boil them for food. They search out the hives full of wild honey and cherish the family goat that produces milk for feta cheese.

Less than a quarter of Greece is arable, and only one-tenth of it is good land—found primarily in two great fertile plains. The Amphissian plain stretches away from the cliffs of Delphi to the sea in a silvery gray-green carpet of gnarled olive trees. The plain of Thessaly, a dusty gold mosaic of crops, is bounded on the northwest by the sheer, dreamlike cliffs of Meteora, where monasteries cling to the peaks like eagles.

The charm of the beautiful but austere landscape of Greece is its unceasing variety. The eye is constantly surprised. A road leading through a grove of spectral olive trees may emerge suddenly on the edge of a cliff, overlooking a bay of mottled turquoises and peacock blues, a sliver of white pebble beach and a rock promontory surmounted by the bone-white columns of a temple to Poseidon.

In spite of the dazzling variety of the Greek landscape, there are no harsh extremes; neither burning deserts nor frozen tundra, mammoth redwoods nor awesome volcanoes. Everything can be taken in and appreciated by the human eye and understanding. The highest mountain is Olympus—only 9,750 feet high compared to the 20,320 feet of Mt. McKinley—but the ancient Greeks were certain that Olympus touched the roof of the world. Nature built Greece on a human scale, and the Greeks followed suit, creating their gods and designing their temples to a human scale. This idea of human proportion as the basic unit totally pervades Greek thought.

Mainland Greece can be divided into seven general areas, and to each one can be attributed distinct characteristics.

The northwest corner, just below Albania, is Epirus, the

poorest section of the country. Some of the villages are so inaccessible that the Slavic invasions never reached them, and the people are as blond as the golden Greeks of antiquity. Dodona, the site of the oldest oracle in Greece, is in Epirus. The prophesying priests, Homer writes in the *Iliad*, "sleep on the ground, go bare, and never cleanse their feet."

South of Epirus is Roumeli, equally mountainous and isolated, except for the western slope, known as Aetolia, which descends toward the Ionian Sea and is rich in history and bountiful in fruits and vegetables. Missolonghi, on a man-made, shallow lagoon, is the major town. Here Lord Byron died of a fever on Easter Monday, 1824, during the war of independence, after a violent thunderstorm. Two years later the town fell to the Turks, whose commander, Ibrahim Pasha, boasted that his soldiers collected 3,000 heads and sent ten barrels of salted human ears to the Sultan in Constantinople as proof of his victory.

Across a narrow gulf below Aetolia is the Peloponnesus, the hand-shaped peninsula where the first great Greek civilizations developed. Steep mountains in the north give way to fertile plains in the southern part, which is called the California of Greece for its valleys of fruit trees and flowers. The "thumb" of the hand is Argolis, one of the earliest inhabited regions of Greece, which boasts many legendary sites: Mycenae, the center of the great civilization chronicled in the Homeric epics; Tyrins, the home of Hercules; and Epidaurus, the "Lourdes" of the ancient world.

The Peloponnesus is separated from the rest of the mainland by the Corinth Canal. On the other side of the canal is Attica, the triangular peninsula in which Athens is situated. Attica is bounded on the north by barren mountains and is not fertile, but the landscape is the true vision of classical beauty. Athens was a cultural and political center for a thousand years, beginning in the sixth century B.C., and is again today the center of Greek life.

To the north and west of Attica lies Thessaly, with its vast fertile plain and massive mountain ranges. In legend it was the home of Achilles and of Jason, who led the Argonauts in search of the Golden Fleece. Thessaly was known in ancient times as the center of witchcraft and magic potions allegedly taught the natives by Medea when she came back with Jason from Colchis. Mt. Olympus, the home of the gods, is in the northern part. On Mt. Pelion, to the east, the centaurs were said to live, and even today the natives of the region claim to see nymphs and satyrs cavorting on its slopes.

Wedged between Thessaly and Yugoslavia is Macedonia. The ancient Macedonians were members of the blond Dorian tribe, and produced Alexander the Great, who conquered most of the known world of his time. Salonica (Thessalonika) is the capital of Macedonia and the second largest city in Greece. It was named after Alexander's sister. About fifty miles southwest of it is Vergina, where a royal tomb was found in 1977 full of golden treasures; it is claimed to be the burial site of Alexander's father, Philip of Macedon.

Thrace is a corridor of land running east from Macedonia to the Turkish border. The army of Alexander passed through Thrace to conquer Asia. According to legend it is the birthplace of Orpheus, and therefore, in a sense, of music. The Eastern influence of the Byzantine period is still strongly felt; in some villages there are men who walk on fire during religious rites.

The islands of Greece are spread out on both sides of the mainland. Most of those in the Aegean Sea on the eastern side are divided into four groups: the Saronic islands, clustered in the gulf that separates Attica from the Pelopon-

nesus; the Cyclades, in the southern Aegean; and Dodecanese, which lie along the Turkish coast east of the
Cyclades; and the Sporades, in the northern Aegean. There
is also Crete, where civilization in the Aegean first blos-
somed, but that is a world of its own, and cannot be fitted
into any group of islands. On the west side of the mainland,
in the Ionian Sea, there are far fewer islands and, except for
lush Corfu, they are less known than those in the Aegean.
The most historic of the Ionian group is Ithaca, home of the
dauntless Odysseus.

The Greek landscape is not like any other. And since
the land is still intimately a part of daily life, to discovering
what is unique about the landscape of Greece will reveal a
great deal about the Greek people.

The landscape can be divided into three elements:
water, land, and light. Each one has more significance in
Greece than we would ordinarily attribute to it. Take water
(*neró*). Visiting gourmets come away from the country babbling about the heady taste of cold water. Remembering his
first day in Greece, Henry Miller wrote: "*The glass of water*
. . . everywhere I saw the glass of water. It became obses-
sional. I began to think of water as a new thing, a new vital
element of life." Knock on the door of the poorest hut in
the most remote province of Greece and its inhabitant, before asking your name, will serve you a glass of water accompanied by the traditional sweet. The water of Greece,
whether you drink it ice cold out of a deep natural spring
or from a small tumbler in an outdoor *cafénion*, tastes unlike water anywhere else. I've tried to define the difference,
and can't, except to say that it tastes more of water—more
like the essence of water.

Natural springs are cherished. Villages grow up around
them, and some of them have a history that begins with
legend. On Mt. Hymettus, just outside Athens, flows the

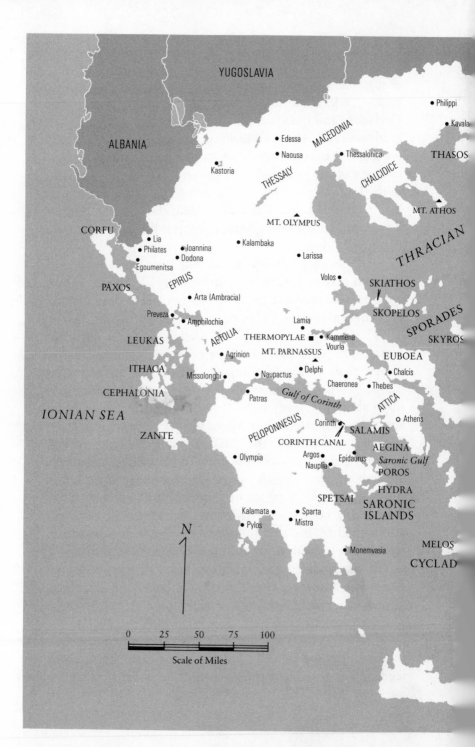

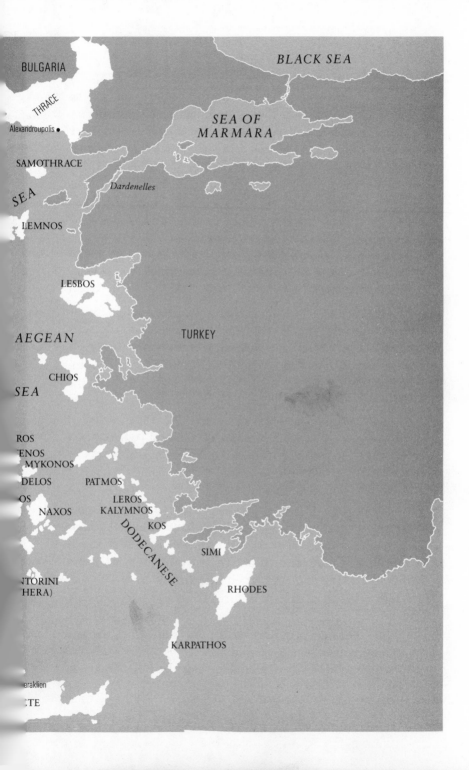

spring that was mentioned in Greek legends for its ability
to increase fertility. Today the spring bubbles out of the
head of a stone ram. A Byzantine monastery was built in-
corporating the spring into its outer walls. The monastery
is deserted now, but on any Sunday the winding road up
the mountain is alive with Athenian families, piled four or
five strong on a motorbike plus sidecar. They come to the
spring to picnic in the shade of the giant old cypresses and
plane trees, and to take home containers filled with the
magic water.

For village women the well or spring is the center of life.
Every crumb of local gossip is shared as they gather there,
just as in Biblical times, filling large clay urns or, more
likely, plastic bottles in fluorescent dime-store colors. Some
women still carry the water jugs home balanced gracefully
on their heads, and they are able to support incredible
weights this way. (The men do their gossiping more com-
fortably while sipping thick sweet Turkish coffee in the
shade of the village plane tree.) From a tumbler of water to
the village well to the sea, water has dictated the quality of
life in Greece. Go as far inland as you can and you are never
more than a day's walk from the sight of the sea. It was by
that sea that the first human inhabitants came to Greece,
and by sea that the island dwellers set out to seek their
fortunes because the land could not support them. Greek
mariners, from the Argonauts to the shipowners of today,
succeeded so well that there are now half as many Greeks
living outside the country as the ten million in it. Every
exile, no matter how great a fortune his new life has
brought him, no matter how forbidding and barren the island of his birth, still remains fiercely Greek. He will talk
for hours, with tears in his eyes, of the land he has left and
of his hopes to return there to die.

Next, the land. It is often said that the basic colors of

Greece are those of its flag: blue and white, and indeed the blue of sea and sky are intoxicating; the sun gives stones and columns and whitewashed huts a painful whiteness. But there is a third basic color to Greece: the red of the soil. It is a dusty brick-red often called Greek red, and it is every-where—the bare dirt, the tiled roofs of the little white houses, the dust on the hands of the farmers, the figures of youths and maidens on ancient Greek urns. The red earth of Greece, held in the embrace of the sea, is one of the three elements that make the Greek landscape unique. To the Greek peasant, this red, dry soil is the hard master from whom he must coax enough food to sustain life. Nearly one-third of all Greeks are still directly involved with tilling the land. The farmer must pry the stones from his field by hand, scrape together decayed leaves to provide nourish-ment for the soil and dig terraces to keep it from washing downhill. Nevertheless, the crops of olives, figs, grapes, wheat, beans, and tobacco that the land provides are not enough to support the Greek people, and food must be imported. When the delicate balance is destroyed, as in times of war, even eating the cats and dogs and rats will not keep the population alive. During the Nazi occupa-tion, when imports were cut off, some 40,000 people in Athens alone died of starvation, and the villagers fared no better.

The land of Greece may be poor, but it is also heart-breakingly beautiful. Nature has carved it into curving bays, dramatic coves, caves with iridescent walls. There are gently rolling hills, dizzying mountain ranges, beaches of perfectly oval white pebbles, sheer needles of rock shot with veins of marble, and flat fields dotted with golden-fleeced sheep. The changes from one type of terrain to another are abrupt and dramatic. The Greek has always been acutely conscious of the beauty of his land, as well as of its poverty. Whenever

you round a bend to discover a high cliff or mountain peak
in a setting of great drama, you will always find a ruined
pagan temple or a Byzantine church or monastery that was
built there to make the most of it.

Today, as in pre-Christian times, the Greek finds himself
intimately tied to the land—its moods and crops and seasonal cycles. No wonder he believed, in Hellenistic times,
that every stream and tree harbored the spirit of a naiad or
a nymph, and no wonder that today he will express his most
abstract thoughts in terms of the land, the soil, and the
seasons. (Many notable examples can be found in the work
of Nobel Prize–winning poets George Seferis and Odysseus
Elytis.) To the most uneducated Greek, the legend of Antaeus, who derived his strength from the earth and died
when Hercules held him above the ground, is readily comprehensible on both a symbolic and a literal level.

The water and the land are dominant themes in the
basic design of life in Greece, but they are only supporting
players to the Greek light (fos). The image is suggested by
the great contemporary Greek writer Nikos Kazantzakis:

> In every Greek landscape . . . the light is the protagonist-
> hero. The mountains, the valley and the sea form the
> arena in which he struggles, or the couch on which he
> reposes. The mountains, the valley, the sea play a sec-
> ondary role. The light is the resplendent Sober Dio-
> nysos who is dismembered and suffers, then rejoins his
> parts and triumphs. The entire scene of Greece seems to
> have come to be just so that he might perform.

The stark land is bathed in a pure and intense light that
has been remarked upon by visitors since Roman times.
Great thinkers and writers have set about the nearly impossible task of trying to describe its effect upon the viewer.
Here are three of the most successful attempts:

Whoever has once seen Greece will carry for ever in his heart the remembrance of a miracle of light. No blinding glare, no blazing colors, but an all-pervading, luminous brightness which bathes the foreground in a delicate glow, yet makes the furthest distances clearly visible.   WALTER F. OTTO, 1949

The first impression of the country, from whatever direction one enters it, is austere. It rejects all daydreams, even historical ones. It is drab, barren, dramatic and strange, like a terribly emaciated face; but it lies bathed in a light such as the eye has never yet beheld, and in which it rejoices as though now first awakening to the gift of sight. This light is indescribably keen, yet soft. . . . One can compare it to nothing except Spirit.
                          HUGO VON HOFMANNSTHAL, 1923

In the dazzling sunlight a detail . . . stands out with hair-raising exactitude such as one sees only in the paintings of the very great or the insane.
      Everything is delineated, sculptured, etched. . . . You see everything in its uniqueness—*a* man sitting on *a* road under *a* tree. . . . Whatever you look at you see as if for the first time. . . . Every individual thing that exists, whether made by God or man, whether fortuitous or planned, stands out like a nut in an aureole of light, of time and of space.   HENRY MILLER, 1941

My own first impression of the light of Greece was that the air had disappeared. It was as if I had always been conscious of a haze; a refraction caused by the air standing between me and the world. Now that haze was gone. Colors become so pure and clear that they are almost audible, but never brash and glaring. Every patch of color glows with a great subtlety of shades. I know of no other land where shadows really are purple and lavender and a dozen other colors as well. Watching a patch of sea go through its rep-

ertory of greens and blues can keep one spellbound for
hours. The vision of Greece's unearthly, spiritual, almost
holy light is not reserved only for those who are looking for
it. Even the objective world of science has to take account
of it. Not long ago I came across an article warning amateur
photographers that the light of Greece can deceive the most
practiced travel photographer; that light meters and filters
and such apparatus cannot be relied upon, and that the only
solution is to take and develop a test roll of film before
exposing the rest.

But for non-photographers, what significance can this
light have? What part has it played in the development of
the Greek people and their culture? There is one similarity
among the descriptions of the light quoted above: each ob-
server suggests that it strips things naked, revealing them to
the eye with total honesty. In fact, the passages bring to
mind descriptions of drug experiences, when common objects suddenly begin to pulse with new significance. Henry
Miller's impression of the Greek landscape is that everything has an "eternal cast" about it. A line from the poetry
of William Blake suggests why: "If the doors of perception
were cleansed everything would appear to man as it is, infinite."

One does not need to be a mystic or a poet to see the
infinite quality that the light of Greece imparts to everything. Henry Miller was right. Figures and objects in the
Greek landscape do seem to stand out with a special vivid-
ness. You constantly find yourself face to face with Every-
man. A fisherman sitting on the sand mending his nets
becomes, in the intoxicating light, all fishermen, The Fisherman. A weather-beaten shepherd with a crook carved in
the shape of a serpent, a single olive tree twisted in anthro-
pomorphic anguish, a hibiscus bush against a white plaster
wall—each one assaults the eye as though it had never seen

a shepherd or tree or flower before; as if the image were, in fact, the essence of all shepherds, trees, and flowers. After experiencing the light of Greece, it is easy to understand Plato's doctrine of the ideal object, of which every other object is an imitation, and to guess how that philosophy was conceived.

Appreciating the quality of this light, which tolerates no half-tones, no secrets, which sets every object ablaze with significance, is the cornerstone to an understanding of Greece. The ancient Greeks found it natural to discover metaphysical meanings in everyday objects, and to personify abstract concepts in physical form. Apollo was the personification of light and of learning. The two were one. Today, as in the past, common objects and happenings have cosmic overtones for a Greek. The curiosity of the Greek, his enthusiasm for new experiences, his tendency to dramatize the smallest incident into high tragedy or comedy— all these are related to his sense of the god behind the man, the eternal truth behind the most humble object. Those who have come to know Greece well often remark that every Greek is a philosopher. Given the land—poor, harsh, cruel, yet beautiful and bathed in the light of the infinite—how could he be anything else?

It is necessary to understand one more thing about the landscape of Greece: it is haunted. Let me say quickly that the greatest disservice one can do to the country is to approach it as a museum, a shrine to a dead civilization. Those who come to worship the classical Greeks and gaze only at their temples miss the real Greece. Nevertheless, from some of the ancient Greek legends we can learn something about the land that is Greece today. Mycenae is an example of the way the land is haunted. In 1863 a middle-aged multimillionaire German merchant and classical scholar, Heinrich Schliemann, made a visit to Greece that changed his life. He

gave up his business to devote himself to proving that the
Iliad was not fiction but fact. He divorced his wife and
married a sixteen-year-old Greek girl. First he dug up the
city of Troy, just where Homer had said it would be. Then
he turned his attention to Mycenae, where the ill-fated
house of Atreus acted out its tragedy. The stones that had
once been the palace were still visible. Digging within the
walls, Schliemann found nineteen ancient graves filled with
treasures of bronze and gold. In the tomb of a king he found
a body with a golden death mask. When he removed the
mask, he discovered that the centuries-old corpse was remarkably well preserved. He sent a telegram to the Greek
king: "Have gazed on face of Agamemnon!" Schliemann
was certain he had proved the truth of Homer's tragic tale
of the house of Atreus. But controversy still surrounds his
work. No one knows whether the tombs are indeed those
of Agamemnon and his family. No one can be certain that
the dark tales of murder, adultery, madness, and cannibal-
ism have any basis in fact.

Nevertheless, Mycenae remains eloquent. Anyone who
has walked among the stones is overcome, for no logical
reason, with the certainty that this is a place of tragedy and
unspeakable evil. Whether Homer was reporting historic
truths or whether the legends grew up to explain the eerie
ambiance of the place does not really matter. Before you
accuse me of an overactive imagination, climb to the top of
Mycenae, which crowns a truncated hill rising from the
Argive plain. I once visited it on a day when the ruins
crouched like bare bones under the breathless heat. On
either side of the hill are two companion hills—small mountains, really. One is lush and covered with grazing goats and
their shepherds. The other is bare, bleak, and gray. There is
something unbelievably tragic in the entire atmosphere surrounding these three lonely hills. I spent a while sitting on

the highest point of the ruins. There was nothing there except stones marking where the foundations of the palace
had been. On one side I could see black goats grazing lazily
below me, looking no bigger than gnats. But the sound of
their bells came through the empty air as clearly as if they
were a few yards away. While I sat there I felt such a sense
of oppressive evil that I could almost hear the screams of
Clytemnestra, Cassandra, and the murdered children.
Whatever structure once stood here, I came away convinced
that to live in it for any length of time would surely lead to
madness. What explanation is there for such a reaction to
an unremarkable collection of rocks? I can only reply that
the landscape of Greece is haunted. I felt it often; many
others have remarked upon it, and the Greeks have always
known it.

Mycenae is not an isolated case. Greece abounds with
sites that seem to have a life of their own—by no means all
tragic. Delphi is an example familiar to many visitors. I have
always been amused by the story of how, more than eight
centuries before Christ, a shepherd on the steep slopes of
Mt. Parnassus had felt a rush of cold air coming out of a
crevice in the earth and had fallen into a divine frenzy,
babbling nonsense. From that time until four centuries after
the birth of Christ, Delphi was the seat of a divine oracle.
About 1000 B.C. it became sacred to Apollo. Sitting where
the sacred breeze washed over her, the priestess would fall
into an ecstasy to answer the questions put to her. Delphi
became a religious, intellectual, and political center. Trea-
suries were built and filled to overflowing with the gifts and
monuments offered by pilgrims hoping for a favorable
prophecy. Among the treasures unearthed was a large con-
ical stone *omphalos* or "navel," set there as a rather crude
witness to the fact that Delphi was considered the navel of
the world.

When I finally set foot on the slopes of Delphi, I stopped laughing at the naïveté of a people who chose this place as the center of the world. The spot where the shepherd discovered the divine current of air is truly the most magnificent natural setting that can be imagined. To try to describe it would be an exercise in futility. While I stood there, the plain far below turned from silver to gray as the sun began to set, and the shadows of the columns crept down the slopes like fingers. The changing of the light was so dramatic that one almost expected to hear an Olympian roll of drums. Even the busload of American senior citizens and the skylarking group of identically dressed orphan boys seemed to be momentarily touched with the spirit of the place. I think that if all traces of man's history were erased, but Delphi itself remained, a passer-by at some future time would again discover divine emanations at the same spot and would declare it to be the center of the world. And perhaps he would be right.

TWO

The Children
of
Gaia

> "Greeks soar but keep their feet
> on the ground."
> GREEK PROVERB

Anyone who has seen a picture or a reproduction of Praxiteles' Hermes knows what Greeks *should* look like. Perhaps that is why visitors arriving for the first time are so disappointed to discover what most Greeks really *do* look like: short, squat, and dark instead of tall and blond with a godlike brow and a straight nose. Greek waiters in New York or London are also short and dark, of course, but with the Acropolis as a backdrop, Greeks of today look, let's face it, out of place.

On further acquaintance, however, modern Greeks begin to look more familiar. There's Plato in a coffee house, arguing politics instead of writing dialogues. There's Odysseus navigating Constitution Square on a motorbike in rush hour. There's Penelope sitting behind a typewriter. In every harbor there are Argonauts; in every home there is joy and tragedy straight out of Aeschylus, Sophocles, and Euripides, and it is expressed with the same classic gestures. Behind the olive skin of the modern Greek beats the heart and the spirit of the ancients: the same restless curiosity, the shrewdness, the love of adventure, the capacity for suffering. He shares the same tendency to use strong words and violent gestures; he has the same warm heart, the disdain for time, and the delight in life lived fully, with all the senses awake.

There are still Greeks whose physical features are hauntingly like those in the museums. They are found particularly in remote villages that escaped foreign incursions. But the Greeks of today are not the children of the Greeks who watched Sophocles and Euripides present their tragedies for the first time. For the most part, modern Greeks are the product of centuries of racial mixing, and the invasions by the Turks, Slavs, Franks, and Italians can be read in their faces. On the other hand, Greek character has survived centuries of foreign rule intact. To a large degree, the environment is what molds a national character and, in Greece, where the technological revolution is just beginning to be felt, the environment has changed little in twenty-five hundred years. One-third of the people in Greece still live in rural areas, and most of the rest have moved to the cities only since World War II. So Greeks, more than most Europeans, are still close to the basic springs of character formation: land and climate.

So pervasive and all-powerful are the land and climate of Greece that to live in the country for any significant period is to become Greek. Even the most reserved foreigner will soon notice that he is beginning to use his hands in conversation; the landscape and climate seem to command self-expression. "Even if the Greeks are annihilated and only one Greek is left in Greece," said writer Pericles Giannopoulos, "he'll teach the conquerors Greek and make Greeks of them. The earth, the stones, the mountains are Greek and make Greeks." The first divinity worshiped by the inhabitants of Greece—before Zeus; before Cronus, the father of Zeus; even before Uranus, the father of Cronus—

was the great earth mother, Gaia, from whom all things, even the gods themselves, are descended.

Just as the land speaks eloquently of Greece's past, it has much to tell us about the Greek people of today. One should stop and let the land and air and light enter the spirit, without first cluttering the mind with information. In such a landscape the senses must be given free rein. But while Greece can nourish the spirit beyond belief, it can deny the body beyond endurance, for the land is as poor as it is beautiful. To survive takes a strong heart and a shrewd mind. Every Greek is as much pragmatist as poet; both artist and artisan, because he cannot survive any other way. Throughout history Greeks have led this double life. Sophocles did not just sit in his courtyard writing dramas. He doggedly pursued a career as an administrator and ultimately was named one of the Council of Ten that governed Athens. George Seferis created his poems while working his way up the pecking order of the Greek diplomatic corps. It is not surprising that a scholarly theologian like Archbishop Makarios of Cyprus also was one of the most cunning political leaders in Europe. It's all part of the Janus-faced Greek character.

The cruel nature of the land also helped to forge the national obsession with hospitality. The Greek attitude toward strangers is called *philoxenia*. The term is difficult to define, but essentially it is the respect every Greek has always had for the wants of strangers and his determination to fill those wants. (The Greek work *xenos* can mean foreigner and guest.)

Good hotels are a recent addition to the Greek landscape. Thirty years ago tourist accommodation in Greece ranked not far above that in emerging African nations today. The traveler in Greece has always been at the mercy of the harsh land, so that in antiquity a tradition of hospitality took root and began to grow. The inhabitants would put the traveler's welfare above their own, and if a family owned only one chicken, it would be served as their guest's dinner. Greeks might spend most of their waking hours trying to outfox their next-door neighbor, or even kill him, but a stranger was a different story. In the ancient tragedies a breach of the laws of hospitality calls down the severest punishments from the gods. If it weren't for these unwritten laws, Odysseus would have never made his way back to Ithaca.

Like many traditions bred of necessity and good sense, *philoxenia* began to get a little out of hand. The Greeks judge themselves and their neighbors by how many points they can score in the hospitality sweepstakes. When all other means of persuasion have failed, a Greek will get his way by threatening, "If you don't do as I say, when I come to your village I won't stay at your house." For a Greek to fail in his duties of hospitality is a mark of shame against himself, his community, and his ancestors, who received their sacred responsibility from the gods themselves.

Greeks are as curious about strangers as they are hospitable toward them. Visitors are often surprised to hear a Greek whom they have just met asking them questions about the size of their income, the frequency of their love-making, their political leanings, and how many times they visit their in-laws. It doesn't really matter how these questions are answered because most Greeks won't believe the replies anyway. The questioner has an answer in mind before he poses the question and if it isn't forthcoming, he'll just shake his head and complain that his listener doesn't trust him enough to tell the truth.

The curiosity of Greeks is equaled by their sense of humor, which is as essential a spice to their conversation as oregano is to Greek food. Greek humor has a cutting edge,

and jokes usually aim to puncture a pose, a lie, or a reputation. This competitive repartee—a verbal one-upmanship
—is a constant pastime for the Greeks. A good example is
the story, supposedly true, of an Athenian politician who
went to a provincial town to make a campaign speech. The
villagers gathered in the square for the entertainment, determined to show him by their heckling that they were no
yokels. The politician began his speech and soon launched
into the campaign promises: "I am a man who keeps his
word," he shouted. "If you vote for me, I promise that I
will build you magnificent new schools."

"But we don't have any children," the crowd yelled
back.

"Then bring me your wives," retorted the politician,
winning the round, "and I will make you children."

Humor is as vigorous today in Greece as it was centuries
ago when Socrates joked about the shape of his nose and
the bad temper of his wife. Socrates aside, however, no
Greek sees anything about himself that is at all funny or
preposterous. Jokes about third parties are welcomed, but
the smallest joke about himself will only make him angry.
The smile that crosses his lips can be misleading. A Greek
smiles not only when he is happy, but when he is angry as
well. There is in every Greek something of the villain played
by Jack Palance in *Shane*, and it has been there throughout
Greek history. In the *Iliad*, Homer describes the fear that
spread through the Trojans when Ajax advanced toward
them, "smiling under his threatening brows."

Just as no Greek will laugh at himself, every Greek is
convinced of his own omniscience. After readily admitting
his limited education and experience, he will proceed to
explain why he is right and everyone else is wrong. Whatever the subject—science, theology, politics, psychology—
every Greek feels he is an expert on it. Every Greek is an

Aristotle. In this age of specialization and science, the Greek attitude may be exasperating to many foreigners, but perhaps it isn't entirely a fault. In a world of anti-heroes, it is encouraging to encounter a nation of men who still believe in the idea of the Renaissance man—that man is the center of the universe.

There are two subjects that are particular obsessions of Greeks—politics and history. Politics, wrote Aristotle, is a combination of experience and history. The view of contemporary history that is impressed on the consciousness of most Greeks is that Greece has been steadfastly loyal to the West, siding with the Allies in both world wars, sending troops to Korea, joining the North Atlantic Treaty Organization and allowing U.S. bases on its soil. But despite such unswerving loyalty, they feel that the Western Allies, and particularly Washington, have repeatedly slighted Greece in favor of its rival, Turkey, which fought against the Allies in World War I and stayed neutral in World War II. As proof that Washington leans toward Turkey, Greeks point out that the United States did nothing to stop the Turkish invasion of Cyprus in 1974, does not condemn Turkish claims on the Aegean, and pours aid into the country that makes it increasingly stronger and a greater threat to Greece.

In view of the national obsession with history, geopolitical realities do not sway a Greek. Tell him that Turkey may be important to the West because of the collapse of Iran, its 600-mile border with Russia, its control of the Dardanelles Straits and its 500,000-man army, and he will reply, "But all that is meaningless if in a crunch Turkey won't back you, and in both world wars it didn't." Such hard-set attitudes make it wise to avoid political discussions with Greeks and to be prepared to hear your country insulted if you find yourself caught up in one, something I rarely witnessed before the Cyprus invasion of 1974.

Such anger toward the West, often fanned by ambitious politicians anxious to manipulate the strong nationalism of Greeks, has tempered some of the warmth Greeks have traditionally shown toward Americans and Britons. In 1973 when we stayed in Greece while I researched a book, my wife and son were given seats on crowded buses, choice fruits and vegetables in grocery stores, and nothing but smiles when they were heard speaking English. By 1979 when I returned to be the *New York Times* correspondent in Athens, some of the smiles had turned to frowns and at a neighborhood street fair a peddler refused to sell my eight-year-old son a rubber animal after learning he was an American. "Your money is no good here," he said.

But such rudeness is rare, especially outside the major tourist centers where the famous Greek hospitality sometimes wears thin during the busy season. For the most part Greeks are easy to get to know and are as spirited conversationalists as any people on earth. In Greece, conversation, word play, even poetry, are as much a national pastime as betting on the soccer scores.

In ancient Greece, Pericles and his generals would spend the night before a major battle analyzing the merits of a certain image in a line of poetry. At a symposium or a drinking party where the rhetoric was more important than the wine, Socrates and other famous Greek philosophers polished their wit on subjects both sublime and silly while the writers of the day, including Plato, faithfully recorded their *bons mots*. Today almost every educated Greek writes verse, and the works of the country's finest poets become best sellers and are set to music by popular composers, often rising to the top of the hit parade. Young Greeks hum tunes based on Odysseus Elytis's major work, *To Axion Esti (Worthy It Is)*, which was set to music by Mikis Theodorakis. Greeks in village coffee houses and outdoor cafés of downtown Athens gather at new symposia to eat, drink, and make lively conversation.

Near Constitution Square in Athens is Floca, a stylish restaurant, where sidewalk tables provide a view of the passing scene. Nearly every day, one of Floca's tables is occupied by a group of Greece's leading intellectuals, including the Nobel laureate, Mr. Elytis, a fellow poet, Nikos Gatsos, and composers like Manos Hadjidakis, who wrote the music for the film *Never on Sunday*. Their noontime discussions range from the philosophical to the frivolous. "Poets need to talk," says Mr. Gatsos, "to hear the language, to play with it." The kind of word play that goes on at Floca's every day has had a part in the current flowering of poetry in Greece. Even Greek businessmen spend their lunch hours discussing subjects that have little to do with commerce. In the plush, dimly lit bar of the Grande Bretagne Hotel, on Constitution Square, Greek shipowners and business tycoons meet every noon to talk, amid glasses of smoky *ouzo* and the click of worry beads. The subject is as likely to be art or philosophy as high finance. "To exercise the tongue and provoke the mind is the most fulfilling pastime of all," says shipowner Demitrios Gratsos.

Greeks have some less charming characteristics. They can be terribly cruel to each other, although rarely to strangers. They are so proud that they will refuse to admit they are wrong, no matter what the consequences. And if they are pushed too far, their quick temper can lead them to violence in the heat of the moment. Throughout their history, they have reached great heights and shameful lows, often within a very short time. In the fifth century B.C. Athenians showed what miracles can be brought about when people willingly work together for the good of all. Thucydides has Pericles say, "We are a free democracy. We do not allow absorption in our own affairs to interfere with participation in the state's. We regard the man who holds himself aloof from public affairs as useless; nevertheless we yield to no one independence of spirit and complete self-reliance." When the great test came with the invasion of Greece by Persia, Athenians showed their mettle. They took the lead in giving battle to the immense forces of the East, and, alone, they won the incredible victory at Marathon that forced the mighty host to depart.

Twenty-four centuries later Greeks performed another miracle when they faced a different invader in the autumn of 1940. Within days after Italian troops began pouring into Greece from Albania, a vastly outnumbered Greek army met the invader head on and, to the astonishment of the world, not only drove them out of the country in a few weeks, but across half of Albania as well. A small force of inadequately armed Greeks destroyed Mussolini's military pretenses once and for all and humiliated the Italian dictator before the world just as their ancestors had humiliated the Persian tyrant 2,400 years earlier. Although the Greek army eventually had to give way before the massive German force that followed the Italians, Greeks showed by their strong resistance to the Nazis and by their victory over the Italians that the spirit of Marathon and Salamis still lived. Hitler was forced to divert to the Balkans troops that were to have taken part in the invasion of Russia, fatally delaying the invasion so that the Germans became bogged down in the long Russian winter. The miraculous victory of the Greeks became a turning point of the whole war.

But, in both ancient and modern times, Greeks moved within a short period from astounding the world by driving out superior forces that had invaded their country to butchering each other in internecine conflicts—the Peloponnesian War in ancient times and the Greek civil war in ours. Thucydides gives a terrible picture of the condition of Greece in the last years of the Peloponnesian War. There were "excesses of savagery" and "monstrous retaliation," he writes. "People dared the most awful deeds at a moment's caprice." Every citizen mistrusted every other; every man feared and hated his neighbor. The very meaning of words was changed. "Moderation was despised as weakness; prudence was cowardice; recklessness and cunning were admirable. That guilelessness which is the chief characteristic of a noble nature was laughed to scorn and disappeared." That graphic picture of the Peloponnesian War also accurately portrays what happened in Greece in the civil war of the 1940s. After the Germans retreated from Athens at the end of 1944, fighting broke out in the capital; Communist extremists launched a bloodbath against real and imagined enemies, executing 13,500 fellow Greeks in less than three weeks. As the French Marxist historian Dominique Eudes writes,

> OPLA, the KKE's [Greek Communist Party's] secret police . . . decided the time had come for the great washing of dirty linen recommended by all Stalinist precepts. They hunted down Mencheviks, Trotskyists, and "social traitors" with as much zeal as they expended on collaborators and war criminals. They represented the abstract revolution eating at the vitals of the Greek revolution like a tapeworm.

In the civil war that lasted into the end of the decade, 125,000 Greeks died at the hands of their countrymen, many innocent civilians executed in excesses of savagery that equaled anything Thucydides described.

When their baser instincts are not given vent by war or political upheaval, however, Greeks are surprisingly slow to violence. Indeed, Greece has one of the lowest rates of violent crime in the world and the lowest in Europe. The rate for murders, for example, averages 1.3 per 100,000 compared with 8.8 in the United States and 3.8 in Italy. In recent years there has been an increase in political assassinations, both by Greek leftist extremists, whose victims have included several Americans, and by Arab terrorists who use Athens as a base of operations. But even acts of terrorism in Greece are below the level of the rest of Europe. Between 1974 and 1984 there were 19 assassinations in Greece by terrorists while during the same period there were 33 in Belgium and 186 in Italy.

The reason for the comparatively low crime rate does not seem to be tough treatment of wrongdoers by either judges or prison officials. "Although capital punishment exists on the books, there has not been a single execution in years," Nicholas Androulakis, professor of criminal law at Athens University told me when I was a correspondent in Athens. "Long prison terms are not frequent.... In the prisons inmates are not expected to work, and those who do have each workday counted as two." The rate of violent crimes has remained fairly consistent except for a period in 1968, when it was even lower. "For about a year everyone apparently held back out of fear of the dictatorship, but by 1969 the rate of convictions had gone back to normal levels," says Mrs. C. D. Spinellis, a lecturer on criminology at the University of Athens Law School who has made a special study of fluctuations in crime rates. She and Androulakis concur in attributing the low rate to strong family and community pressures. "Greece remains a traditional society, where family and community ties are still very strong," Mrs. Spinellis says. "There is little anonymity here. When you know your neighbor, you don't harm him, because you need him. Studies in criminality show that informal controls, such as the family and the communtiy, are the most effective controls."

Alexander Lykourezos, a criminal lawyer, recalled that

almost every one of his clients who was involved in a felony was more concerned about his family's reaction to his crime than about the judge's reaction. "The usual family response," he says, "is, 'How could you bring such shame on the family?'—not, 'Why did you do it?' or 'How have we failed you?' A response like that from people you care about is the most effective deterrent there is." Crime statistics bear out this theory. "The incidence of those crimes condemned by the community—rape, murder, robbery—are very low in Greece, but those crimes not popularly considered reprehensible, like white-collar crime and tax evasion, which is endemic here, are quite high," Androulakis explains. As for organized crime, Mrs. Spinellis said the few incidents of criminals working in conjunction with each other have involved the selling of narcotics and the stealing and smuggling of antiquities.

Although family and community strictures may be keeping Greece among the more trouble-free nations, the flood of people moving from small villages into the urban centers is creating anonymity, which is slowly undermining those strictures. According to Mrs. Spinellis, juvenile delinquency and narcotics arrests are slowly increasing. "We're fortunate right now, but we're being extensively urbanized and I'm afraid our low crime rate won't last long," she said.

Greeks have as many faults and virtues as most peoples, but the mixture, extensively stirred over four thousand years, is as unique as their land. The average Greek sees himself as two people. He is sure that there flows in his veins some of the blood of his noble ancestors, the ancient Greeks, but he is just as certain that there are in him plenty of negative characteristics inherited from the barbarians who followed. He even calls himself by different names to distinguish the two opposing personalities. When he feels noble, courageous, or creative, he calls himself a *Hellene*, which is the word for Greek that was used even before Pericles' time. When he feels devious, obstinate, or selfish, he calls himself a *Romios*, which is the Greek word for Roman. The part of him searching the stars is Hellenic; the part fighting for position in the dirt is Romaic.

The reason for the distinction goes back many centuries. After the decline of Rome, the eastern capital of the empire, Constantinople, prospered as the center of Byzantium. Although the culture and language of the empire were Greek, the administration was Roman and every citizen in the empire called himself a Roman. To the Turks, who were moving steadily toward Constantinople, the empire was known as Rum. After Constantinople fell to the Turks in 1453, all Greeks under Ottoman rule were called, in Islam, *Rumis*, and every Greek used the word *Romios*, the Greek form of *Rumis*, when referring to himself or to any of his countrymen. To keep their national identity intact over the ensuing four centuries of Turkish subjugation, Greeks had to use all the strength, cunning, and deviousness they could muster. Then, after winning independence in 1831, Greeks looked back to their ancient greatness and, as they struggled to recover a proper place in European civilization, consciously tried to encourage qualities in themselves that were Hellenic. But at every step of the way they were forced to fight the strongly Romaic aspects in their nature.

The Romaic side of today's Greek focuses on the real and the possible, evaluates achievements in terms of money and power, relies on instinct in making decisions, distrusts and tries to bypass the law, values learning as a means of advancement, loves folk music and dance, feels strong loyalty to the native region, and will consider any compromise to gain personal ends. The Hellenic side focuses on the ideal, evaluates achievement in nonmaterial terms, relies on logic, respects the law and will not bypass it on principle, respects learning for its own sake, prefers European music and dance, loves Athens more than any other region, and abhors compromise in any form.

The one feeling shared by the Romaic and the Hellenic nature of the Greek in exactly the same measure is love of country. The threat of an invasion or the destruction of their country will unite all Greeks and inspire them to such acts of bravery as to make the gods weep. During World War II Greeks fought as fiercely and as courageously against the Italians and the Germans as their ancestors had against the Persians twenty-five centuries earlier.

Greeks love their country so much that they have a word for their state of being when they are away from her —*xenitia*. The word has no English equivalent, but Elias Kulukundis, in his book *The Feasts of Memory*, gives the best definition I know: "It is . . . not exactly exile because it can be self-imposed, and not estrangement because there is no spiritual estrangement. *Xenitia* is simply the loss of the native land." Even though Greeks have had to leave their native soil through the centuries in order to survive, the loss they feel never subsides in its intensity. There is a Greek saying that expresses it well: "The most painful experiences a Greek can know are to be an orphan, to be alone, to be in love, and to be away from Greece. And to be away from Greece is the worst of all."

THREE

A Way of Life

> "A woman should be everything in the
> house and nothing outside it."
> EURIPIDES,
> *Meleager*

As in most western countries, the winds of women's liberation and the sexual revolution have had a dramatic impact on the roles and rights of women in Greece. In the past few years laws have been passed that have dramatically improved their lot: abortion has been legalized, divorce has been made easier, women may keep their maiden names after marriage, the need to pay a dowry to a husband has been made illegal, and women are being welcomed into many professional fields. Nevertheless, the practice of equality for women is still lagging behind in a country that, while geographically in Europe, has long felt the pull of the Orient in terms of women's roles. For instance, until recently it was considered a blot on a husband's masculinity and ability to provide if his wife was obliged to work, and many women who are now employed make elaborate excuses as to how they don't really *need* to work but only do it as sort of a hobby.

Women at every level of Greek society are brought up to coddle their men. This is dramatized when a visitor attends a buffet dinner at a Greek home even in the most sophisticated salons of Athens. When the hostess announces that dinner is ready, the men continue talking as if they were all deaf while the women spring to their feet and line up at the buffet table to assemble a plate of delicacies not for themselves but for their husbands and escorts. Then they carry the groaning plate to their man and sit beaming, coaxing them to eat. Only later will the women feed themselves. Many Westerners are bemused to see that at any Greek gathering the women and men inevitably gravitate to opposite sides of the room. Often the women will disappear entirely into the kitchen where they spend the evening cooking and gossiping while the men decide the fate of the world in the living room.

Nevertheless, the plight of women in Greece is slowly improving. A woman can marry without a dowry, adultery is no longer a criminal offense, arranged marriages are becoming rare and couples can have either civil or church weddings, although the vast majority still consider a church marriage the only binding contract. Few Greek men still insist on virgin brides or will send home a bride who has not convincingly proved her virginity on her wedding night. Even in the most remote villages the practice of hanging out a blood-stained wedding sheet is a distant memory. But once married, a Greek woman is expected to put her husband and her male children first at all times, and even the semblance of flirtation earns her universal censure, while the romantic adventures of married males are looked on with amused tolerance.

In a dramatic departure from only a few decades ago, education is encouraged nearly as much for women as for men, and half of Greek women now work outside the home (although few Greek women, especially in the upper classes, feel constrained to have a "career" to justify their existence). The responsibility of looking after the family and the home is still borne overwhelmingly by women, however, even if they work. When they finish their job, they are expected to come home and manage the household with no help from their husbands. The most prized jobs for women are in the civil service or in government-owned enterprises because they are overstaffed, the workload is light, and the workday ends at 2:30 P.M. so women don't come home too tired or too late to cook and clean. Furthermore, it is constitutionally impossible to get fired from a civil service job. Therefore, such a position has replaced the dowry of money or property as the most valuable asset a single girl can bring to a marriage.

Marriage and a family take precedence over careers for all but a few, and women are measured by others and value themselves in terms of what they accomplish at home as mothers and homemakers rather than by what they achieve at work. In some villages the women still plant and harvest, tend the sheep, and carry the heavy loads while the men sit under plane trees sipping coffee and playing cards. Throughout Greece the coffee house is still primarily a male environment where a woman would draw as many stares as she would if she walked down the main street of the village wearing trousers. But Greek women are not weak-willed. Because the administration of the home is left entirely to them, they learn to make decisions and to use the limited power they have. Like all oppressed groups, they use their weakness as a weapon, getting their way by complaints, sighs, and tears rather than demands and ultimatums. And if the situation calls for courage, Greek women have repeatedly, throughout their history, demonstrated their ability to bear great hardship for home and family and have even become some of Greece's most celebrated warriors on the battlefield.

The role of wife is still vastly preferred by Greek women

to being single, and the number of couples living together without benefit of marriage is so small that it is not yet measurable. Family and community pressures remain very strong in Greece and any woman taking such a step would not only be criticized for her morals but would be considered a fool by practically everyone she knows.

Few Greek women feel they have fulfilled their role in life until they have produced a son. "May you have male children and female sheep" is a standard Greek blessing. This was true even in ancient Greece. As Sophocles wrote, "Sons are the anchors of a mother's life." The male child is a woman's crowning achievement and she regards him as a god. Daughters in a Greek home quickly learn their inferior place in the universe. The son is a king and the women are his slaves. The bondage of Greek girls begins in the nursery and is well taught by another woman, their mother. A Greek wife is loyal and loving, but she takes more pride in the achievements of her son than in those of her husband because her husband was, after all, created by another woman. She rules her son the way she influences her husband—through weakness. Her tears, her sighs, her silent suffering are all powerful weapons to which Greek men usually capitulate.

It is as a mother that the Greek woman achieves respect, power, and love. No wonder she is in such a hurry to get married and bear children. The mother is sacred in Greece. The worst insult to a Greek is a disparaging remark about his mother. There have been cases of Greeks literally getting away with murder by proving that they were provoked to violence by insults to the reputation or memory of their sainted mother. What keeps the mother–son bond from having a crippling effect on the personality of Greek boys is the strong role of the Greek father. A dominating, powerful figure in the home, he is an irresistible model from which

Greek boys develop a strong masculine identity of their own.

The hierarchy of power in the Greek family may be readily observed on any street during spring and summer evenings. In the warm months Greek families go out almost every night, to a corner taverna perhaps, or just for a *peripato* (promenade). Greeks hate being alone inside their houses. They are always going somewhere, or just strolling, stopping often along the way to chat with friends, neighbors, or relatives. In these little outings, the husband always walks slightly ahead, fingering his worry beads (*komboloyia*) without bothering to look sideways to see if his wife and children are obediently following. He has no reason to look. They could be nowhere else, because centuries of tradition and the father's overpowering personality have made them extensions of himself.

The only exception to the universal dominance of the male occurs in the small village of Monoclissia in Macedonia every January 8. On this day the sexes reverse their roles. The women leave the housework behind, and smoke cigarettes as they stroll through the streets, or sit in the village café drinking and debating local politics. The men are obliged to take care of the children, the cooking, and the chores. If a man appears outside the house, according to the local tradition, he becomes a prisoner of the women and is subjected to mysterious, painful punishments. This strange rite goes back to pre-Christian times and is even featured in one of the comedies of Aristophanes. This one moment of glory aside, the majority of Greek women consider the dominance of the male as part of the natural order. Even names of his children reflect the husband's importance. The first son is always named after the father's father, and only if there is a second son is the mother allowed to name it after her father. My father, for example, was named

Christos after his father's father. I was named Nicholas after my father's father, and my son was named Christos after my father.

In the rearing of children, the father is responsible for discipline and the mother is responsible for everything else. Because Greeks put a great deal of emphasis on it, most children are carefully dressed and well behaved in public. They make sure to address strangers in the formal, rather than the familiar form, and no matter how well they get to know their elders they always employ a title, such as *Kyrie* (Mr.) or *Thie* (Uncle), before the name. Children do not move out of the family home as long as they are single. Although several young men may jointly rent a small apartment—a *garçonnière*—where they can entertain and generally sow their wild oats, they continue to eat and sleep at their parents' homes.

But though men share practically none of the housework and little of the childcare, they do look upon their families as the center of their lives and their homes as their kingdoms. They would rarely consider uprooting their families to move to another city for a better job, and if they have to leave home for economic reasons—to earn a living on ships or as guest workers in other countries—they choose to leave the family behind, surrounded by a support system of relatives and neighbors, rather than to disrupt their status quo by transplanting them. Men take full responsibility for dealing with family crises. They rarely sacrifice their family life for their ambitions. They don't drink excessively and if they do have an occasional sexual adventure they don't let it become an emotional entanglement that might threaten their marriage. They don't talk much about their work because they tend to regard it as a means of earning a living and not a source of satisfaction. As a result most of them are concerned about how they can make the most money for the least amount of effort rather than how interesting a job might be. But they are not reticent about discussing their family and they take great pride in their homes because the home provides the emotional rewards they most value.

A visitor to a Greek home is always greeted with great warmth, often with an embrace and a kiss on both cheeks. The men stay with the guest and the women serve everything, including the drinks. The evening begins with a glass of water and a sweet—a pastry such as *baklava*, or a fruit preserve. Every housewife keeps these "spoon sweets" on hand for unexpected guests, and they are always some sort of syrupy candied fruit made by boiling together equal weights of sugar and fruit. Any of dozens of kinds of fruit are used, and occasionally even soft walnuts or tiny tomatoes. The sweets are served in a bowl on a special treasured tray—as magnificent as the family can afford—that has notches for spoons. The oldest guest is served first. He takes a spoonful of the sweet, then lifts his glass of ice cold water. Before sipping it he expresses a formal good wish to his host and hostess, such as "*Yiasas*" ("To your health"). Then the sweet is eaten. After that a drink is served. It is usually *ouzo*, but Greeks keep other liquor around and offer it proudly.

Greeks are always pleased by compliments on the appearance of their home. The women spend hours preparing the house for a visit and they are sorely disappointed if nothing is said. But compliments need to be phrased carefully. If a visitor admires a single object, some Greeks will insist on giving it to him no matter how much they prize it. On a summer weekend a few years ago I was driving through western Greece toward Epirus with a fellow journalist, Stanley Penn, and his wife and two children. We stopped for a rest at Amphilochia, a small town on the

Ionian Sea. I remembered that it was the home of a family distantly related to one of my brothers-in-law so, after making a few inquiries, I led the Penns to the house. My distant relative, Tasso Bartzokis, is a tinsmith who lives above the shop in which he sells pans, kettles, and skillets that he creates himself in an old-fashioned forge. Mr. Bartzokis and his wife received our unexpected visit with all the enthusiasm of true Greek hospitality, even though we had appeared during the siesta. They offered us sweets, *ouzo*, and Greek coffee and begged us to stay for dinner and to sleep in their home. "We can go to a neighbor's and the house will be yours," Mrs. Bartzokis said. "Please stay." We demurred politely but firmly, pleading an appointment that night in Ioannina, but the Penns bravely ate every bit of the large candied plum in sugar syrup that was given to each of us.

Before we left, Mr. Bartzokis was delighted to show the Penns and their children the shop where he hand-hammered and polished copper pots. The Penns admired many of the heavy, expensive pieces and Mr. Bartzokis tried to make them a present of each one they mentioned. They were dismayed because they realized that each pot represented hours of work and a much-needed source of income. But Mr. Bartzokis refused to let us out the door until he was allowed to give their little daughter one of the small copper kettles she admired. The kettle, filled with straw flowers, now sits in the living room of the Penns' Manhattan apartment, a shining example of Greek hospitality. (Children, incidentally, are one of the few permissible gambits for repaying Greek hospitality. Like all doting parents, Greeks love to hear their children praised, and if a foreign visitor stuffs some money into the children's hands, no matter how small the child, the parents will not be insulted, for Greek visitors often salute their host's children this way.)

Beyond their children, Greeks maintain strong ties to an

extended family unit that includes parents and sisters and brothers, uncles and aunts, nephews and nieces, cousins, and in-laws. Many Greeks, in fact, feel degrees of obligation to non-relatives from their native village, district, and even province, which they call *patrida*—fatherland. When two Greek strangers strike up a conversation, they first try to determine if they could be even remotely related, or at least whether they are an acquaintance of a relative. One will examine the other shrewdly, then demand, "Are you an Epiroti [native of Epirus]?" "No, I am Thracian, but my cousin's sister-in-law married an Epiroti from [the village of] Mavroneri." Often whole factories in Athens are filled with employees from the owner's province.

In the Greek family each member has definite responsibilities, and the roles are very different from those in an American family. If the father has money, the children don't have to wait until he dies to get their share. Daughters get much of it when they marry, often in the form of a house or apartment or furniture, and sons get it as soon as they start their careers. If the parents are poor, the sons contribute their earnings. Few old people live alone in Greece. A child's duty is to share his home with his parents as long as they live, and the old people are respected and useful members of the family. Their voice is listened to in family councils and they have household tasks to perform. To put one's parents in a home for the aged, or even to allow them to live alone in the family home, would invite the censure of the community. This strong loyalty to family and distant relatives, even to neighbors in the same province, goes back to the harsh, unfruitful land. No man can work it alone. He needs the support of his sons and daughters and relatives. A man grows quickly old and helpless because of a hard life, so the culture perpetuates a tradition of caring for one's elders.

In spite of the strong ties, love and harmony do not always reign in the Greek family. Greeks are emotional and quick to anger, and they quarrel frequently and with great passion. In many families half the members are usually not talking to the other half. But grudges do not last long—a few days at most. In Athens in 1968 I got embroiled in a political discussion with a cousin. Within minutes he was inundating me with the most damning epithets I had ever heard. Finally he called his entire family into the room, seated them in a circle and, pointing at me in a gesture of righteous anger, announced to his audience, "When I die, if you allow this man to attend my funeral, my curse will be on all of you for as long as you live." Understandably, I did not call again at his house soon, and I was surprised to have him stop by my hotel a few days after the argument. "Where have you been?" he asked. "We thought maybe you had gone back to America."

"You told me you never wanted to see me again," I reminded him.

He looked at me with exasperation. "You know," he said, "a friend of mine told me I shouldn't discuss politics with you Americans. You're all too damn sensitive."

If Greek men are acutely sensitive about anything, it is their virility. It is best to nod agreeably when they start to talk about their success with the opposite sex. They boast that as lovers they have such superior skills that men of other nations pale by comparison, and they offer as proof the hordes of unattached Northern European women who flock to Athens, Rhodes, Mykonos, and Corfu every summer for their attentions. There are groups of young Greek men who make a career of pursuing such visitors; they are called *kamaikia* (harpoons). The harpoons are not strictly gigolos because they don't take money for their sexual services, expecting only the rewards of free food and entertainment, a few gifts, and the gratitude of their foreign companions; but they are a closely organized subculture with very specific rules of dress and behavior. The harpoons believe they are providing such an important service to the national economy that a few years ago they threatened to organize into a labor union.

The reputation of Greek women as lovers is naturally not discussed as much as the erotic skills of the men. In a culture where a woman's chastity is still prized, where until recently many girls were not allowed to go out alone with a man unless formally engaged, it is hard to see how they could perfect their skills as lovers, but there are many who claim they are in no way inferior. Lawrence Durrell, the British poet and novelist who lived in Greece for many years, summed up the Greek woman as lover in an essay on Mediterranean women:

> She is destined to be a wife and she knows it and accepts. She is *born* to be a lover. . . . She can let her sensuality overturn a whole world if it is given free rein, but on the other hand she can become an anchorite because no other men (except the one she loves) seem worth loving. It is this comprehensiveness of her passion which can inspire great poets, can inspire men to become eunuchs for her sake. (That is why she is dangerous to the ordinary run of men.) In fact, she was born to sire poets. . . .

FOUR

Can We Talk?

"It is Greek; it can't be read."
(Graecum est; non potest legi.)
MEDIEVAL LATIN SAYING

For a long time foreigners have given the Greek language the reputation of being hopelessly difficult for anyone who didn't learn it as a child. This reputation is not really deserved. When one considers the complexities of German noun endings, French irregular verbs, and Latin prepositions, not to mention the vagaries of English spelling and pronunciation, Greek appears to be one of the more logical European languages. In one way, however, it does live up to its grim reputation. Generations of Greek schoolchildren have been driven to distraction by having to learn one kind of Greek for church, another for formal proclamations and invitations, another for reading newspapers, and a fourth for talking and for reading modern literature. The visitor to Greece need be concerned with only one of these—the colloquial modern Greek called demotic (from *demos*, "people"), which is spoken in the streets and used by modern authors. He can put aside the thought of church Greek, formal Greek, and ancient Greek.

What makes the language seem most formidable to the foreigner is its odd-looking alphabet. Furthermore, most

53

Greek words sound quite unlike their equivalents in better known Romance or Germanic languages. Many visitors give up completely the moment they learn that the Greek work for "no" is *ochi* and the Greek word for "yes" is *ne*. So they spend their time in Greece relying on sign language and hoping devoutly that most Greeks speak either English or French. And indeed, in the cities older people of the wealthier classes generally speak fluent French and many young people are now taught English. Even in the remotest villages there is generally one venerable fellow who learned English forty years previously in the stockyards of Chicago or the kitchen of a New York hamburger joint, and who is delighted to show it off. Greeks are so theatrical and so full of curiosity about strangers that sign language alone will go farther here than anywhere else.

There is no need to worry about the Greek alphabet while driving. On highways, traffic signs are written both in Greek and in Roman letters, and traffic policemen wear flag symbols indicating which foreign languages they speak. Greek traffic police tend to have split personalities: they are superhumanly patient with foreigners, but when their captive audience is a fellow Greek, they will usually erupt into a fiery display of histrionics that would warm the heart of Medea. (Moral: there are times when a fluent command of Greek is best forgotten.)

Anyone ignorant of the Greek alphabet need not fear starvation. Even small restaurants that are frequented by tourists usually have a mimeographed menu in several languages, including English and French. Not everything on these ingenious menus is available every day; only those dishes that have a price inked in next to them can be ordered. (The menus, however, while fascinating reading, are not always helpful. At one charming outdoor restaurant in the resort town of Vouliagmeni, for instance, the outstanding dish was succulent, tiny fried squids, called *kalama-rakia*, but on the menu these were mysteriously translated into English as "ink stands.") And if there is no English-language menu available, there's still no need to go hungry. Throughout Greece it is perfectly acceptable in both humble and fashionable restaurants to go directly into the kitchen and choose one's meal from the pots on the stove. I have fond memories of a magnificent lobster, eaten at a table by the fairy-tale harbor of Hydra, under the steady gaze of half the island's cats. But before I won the lobster of my choice for lunch, I had to pursue it out the door of the restaurant's kitchen and halfway across the dining room.

Still, a foreigner who never ventures a word of Greek will miss a great deal. For one thing, he will miss the sensation caused by his stumbling efforts to communicate. Hearing their own language, however mangled, emerging from a foreigner, overwhelms Greeks with delight and apprecia-tion. The stranger is considered a wonder on the order of Dr. Johnson's dog, who could walk on its hind legs: it is not a matter of how well he does it, but that he does it at all. Friends and neighbors will be called in to hear this paragon of learning. The Greek host will then trot out his own few words of English to return the courtesy. (Greeks are very shy about speaking English if they don't speak it very well. They like to do things perfectly or not at all. But many Greeks who insist that they don't know a word of English *understand* it all too well.) The national delight at hearing a foreigner speaking Greek is a refreshing contrast to touristic experiences in other countries, for example, the widely held French attitude that no foreigner can ever hope to speak French properly, so it would be better if he didn't even try. Surrounded by good will and ready appreciation, a visitor to Greece should make the effort to dip at least one toe into the language. He will be amply rewarded.

An hour spent with a dictionary or phrase book at a sidewalk café is enough to master the Greek alphabet. There are twenty-four letters, from alpha to omega. Ten of the capital letters (A, B, E, Z, I, K, M, N, O, T) and nine of the script or lower-case letters (α, β, δ, ε, ι, κ, μ, ο, τ) look and behave pretty much the way they do in English. There are a few letters that look perfectly familiar but act quite differently from their English counterparts (H, P, Y, X). The rest look at first like hieroglyphics (Γ, Δ, Θ, Λ, Ξ, Π, Σ, Φ, Ψ, Ω). In any case, the beginner has to teach himself only about fourteen new letters, and the job is easier than it is in English because, as a rule, each letter has only one sound.

The rewards of mastering the Greek alphabet are immediate and impressive. Without learning a single complete word, one can distinguish between two theater marquees offering Τζων Γουιην (John Wayne) and Μερυλ Στριπ (Meryl Streep). The last name of Charlton Heston is deliberately misspelled in its Greek form as Easton, because the word *heston* is a scatalogical curse. Formerly inscrutable signs and billboards, as if by magic, transform themselves into familiar entities such as "bar," "cabaret," "Coca-Cola," and "Nescafé." Also, by knowing the alphabet, a stranger can tell whether or not he's on the street he was looking for simply by reading the street sign. From phonetic reading, it is an easy step to learning the useful difference between εξοδος (*exodus*, or "exit") and εισοδος (*isodos* or "entrance"). A great many Greek words, once they are translated, are easy to remember because they form the roots of related English words. For instance, *pente* means five, *octo* is eight, *anthropos* is man, *domatio* is room, *chroma* is color, *micros* is small, *megalos* is large, *cardia* is heart. Almost all scientific, medical, and technical words in English are so closely related to the Greek that they scarcely need translating.

tion of the Gospel into demotic Greek caused rioting in the streets of Athens, and in 1903, when a troupe of players presented Aeschylus's *Oresteia* in demotic Greek, several student spectators died at the hands of soldiers in the fight that ensued. Until recently *katharevousa* was used only for legal documents, parliamentary bills, public notices, formal invitations, and traditional shop signs. But demotic is now the official language, written as well as spoken, although the more learned and traditionalist Greeks may sprinkle their conversations with occasional polysyllabic words of *katharevousa*.

Naturally the demotic could not help absorbing words from the languages of the country's many conquerors. Indeed, it is surprising that the number of foreign words is as small as it is. Nevertheless, loan words from Latin, Italian, Turkish, French, and, since the mid-nineteenth century, English, can be found in modern Greek.

How different is ancient Greek from modern Greek? Some scholars say that a fair comparison is the difference between modern English and the Middle English of Chaucer. Others say that the two are more closely related. No one knows exactly how ancient Greek was pronounced, but many believe that vocal pitch, rather than stress, was used to differentiate between syllables. Today Greek is pronounced in quick, short, distinct syllables of equal length, and only one syllable is stressed in each word. Visitors are often disillusioned to learn that modern Greek has changed so much since the classical age. When a Greek reads the ancient poetry today, it does not even scan properly, and those Greek tragedies that are presented annually in the very amphitheaters where they were first performed have been rendered into modern Greek to make them comprehensible to the audience.

During the Turkish occupation, when Greek literature

and the formal study of the language were stifled, a rich oral tradition developed. Even today, Greeks are unsurpassed storytellers, and their everyday language is rich in proverbs, myths, legends, dramatic gestures, and humor. Even the most uneducated Greek sprinkles his speech liberally with proverbs, many of them reflecting the wry cynicism of a people who have become accustomed to hardship, yet have managed to retain their spiritual strength and sense of humor. The proverbs deal with poverty stoically: "A shoe from home [is best], even if it's patched"; "A bean at a time will fill your sack"; "Prepare an egg, there are nine of us." They explain human nature with good-humored cynicism: "I want to become a saint but the demons won't let me"; "I taught him how to swim and he tried to drown me"; "Only from fools and children will you learn the truth." Another reason for the many proverbs found in ordinary Greek conversation is the national characteristic discussed earlier: the ability to see every incident as representative of the universal condition. What is a proverb, after all, but a universal truth? And the smallest happening—meeting a friend, celebrating a birthday, preparing a meal—is likely to turn a Greek into a philosopher.

Greeks have often used their wit and their humor as a kind of passive resistance to whatever dictatorial government held them in bondage. After the colonels came to power in 1967, strict censorship prevented any criticism of them in Greek newspapers; but within a matter of months after the coup everyone was familiar with hundreds of jokes making fun of the junta. A Greek only had to mention part of one of the punch lines, and everyone at his neighborhood café would chuckle at the shared joke. (All politicians who followed the colonels to power have inspired their own derisive anecdotes, in keeping with a Greek political tradition going back to Pericles, who was called "Squill-head" because of a disproportionately long cranium and who became so sensitive about it that he insisted that all his statues show him wearing a helmet.)

Another characteristic of a language with a rich oral tradition is the widespread use of gestures. Some, particularly the more vulgar ones, are universally understandable. Others can be a bit confusing. Instead of shaking his head "no," a Greek will raise his eyes heavenward, usually with an upward lift of his chin. Naturally, English-speaking visitors frequently mistake this pantomimed "no" for an affirmative nod, especially when it is accompanied by the Greek negative *ochi*, which sounds a bit like "okay." The pantomime of spitting—really just a puff of breath through pursed lips—is used to ward off the jealousy of the evil eye after a compliment has been given or received. When someone does offer good wishes for a particularly hoped-for event, the recipient murmurs, "From your lips to the ear of God."

It is little wonder that the Greeks are fiercely proud of their language. When all the other tongues of Europe were young, Greek had already produced great literature and philosophy. (The Greeks coined the word "barbarian" from a scornful imitation of the ba-ba sounds made by all non-Greek languages.) In spite of centuries of repression, Greek managed to survive when Latin, almost as old and venerated, became a dead language, mummified in church ceremony. In this century, with the burgeoning popularity of Kazantzakis, Elytis, Cavafy, and Seferis, international recognition is finally being given to the renascence of Greek literature. Today Greek still pulses with the same vitality it had in the days of Euripides and Sophocles, and even in this age of technology (*teknologia*), psychiatry (*psychiatria*), and the Greeks still have a word for it.

FIVE

A History of Shadows and Lightning

> "Like a warm and mighty river Hellenism
> with its archons flows."
> Ion Dragoumis

Ten ages make up the recorded history of Greece; some brief and brilliant like flashes of lightning, others long and dark and oppressive. The modern period was preceded by more than four hundred years of Turkish rule, which ended with the revolution of 1821. Before that were the Frankish period, the Byzantine, the Roman, the Hellenistic, the Classic, the Doric, the Mycenaean, and the Minoan.

Greek civilization first flowered more than two thousand years before Christ on the island of Crete, where Minoan kings ruled a powerful maritime empire. These kings, who were at the height of their power about the time of the pharaohs in Egypt, reigned over a dark, Mediterranean race far different from the golden Greeks who succeeded them. The Minoans were an intelligent people, and they attained a high degree of civilization. The palace of Minoan kings at Knossos, for example, contains remnants of a highly sophisticated system of running water with a network of pipes carefully tapered to prevent clogging. And in the queen's bathroom there is a water closet with a flushing system, a bath with a built-in sponge rail, and even an apparatus resembling a bidet.

The Minoans observed an Eastern religion that revered bulls, and it is from this period that the legend of the Minotaur, half-man and half-bull, comes to us. The legend is well known. Theseus, the young Athenian prince, sailed to Crete with a band of youths and maidens—the human tribute that Athens paid annually to the Minoan King Minos. The Athenians would then be devoured by the Minotaur, who lived in a vast Labyrinth. Helped by the king's daughter, Ariadne, Theseus went into the Labyrinth, slew the monster, and retraced his steps by following the string that Ariadne had given him, which he had tied to the entrance.

Like most legends the story has a historical basis. By the fifteenth century B.C., the Minoan empire was overextended. Theseus, king of Athens, tired of having to pay tribute to Crete, raided Knossos while the Minoan fleet was in Sicily. He killed Minos, married Ariadne, and sacked the city. The Labyrinth is thought to have been the palace of Knossos itself, which was decorated throughout with the *labrys,* the double-ax symbol of the Cretans' religion.

Minoan power declined rapidly during the fourteenth century B.C. before the growing strength of Mycenae. The Mycenaeans were an Aryan people from the north who had established a principality in the Peloponnesus, based on a hilltop fortress overlooking the Argive plain (it was in this fortress, according to Homer, that Agamemnon was slain by his wife Clytemnestra and her lover Aegisthus "like an ox of the manger"). The Mycenaeans extended their commercial and military power throughout the mainland and the island, including Crete, but while absorbing Cretan culture, they retained their own language, an early form of Greek.

The Mycenaean period was the age of heroes and of the Trojan War. The story, told in Homer's *Iliad* and Virgil's

Aeneid, is nowadays accepted as largely historical, even if the siege of Troy by Agamemnon and his allies—such figures as Menelaus, Nestor, Odysseus—was undertaken for commercial reasons rather than to avenge the rape of Menelaus's wife Helen by Paris, son of Priam, king of Troy. The Trojans, who controlled the Hellespont, were resisting Mycenaean expansion to the east. (The name Agamemnon means "the most resolute," and was probably a generic title for Mycenaean leaders. The story of Agamemnon's murder is believed to be based on a twelfth-century feud between rival dynasties.)

The Trojan War so weakened Mycenae and its allies that one by one they fell before invading Doric tribes, another northern people, who pushed down through the mainland, driving the Achaeans eastward and destroying their cities, plunging Greece into a dark age that lasted for three centuries. Now came the first example of that remarkable ability so often demonstrated in the long and painful history of Greece, not only to survive conquest but to win over the conquerors themselves. During the Doric period, the creative light lit by the Minoans and nurtured by the Achaeans was diminished but not snuffed out. By the eighth century B.C., the darkness had lifted from most of Greece, except for a few areas like Sparta, where the stark Doric way of life went on for another four hundred years. In the next three centuries, kingdoms broke up into independent city-states. Autocracy gave way to oligarchy and ultimately to democracy. The center of power shifted from the palace to the *agora*, the market place, and glorification of rulers changed to concern for the dignity of the individual. These changes set the stage for what has been called "the Greek miracle." In the golden age that followed, philosophy, literature, and art reached heights that no later age has surpassed.

The main setting for this miracle was Athens. Built on a

plain surrounded by mountains, it was settled by Achaeans fleeing the Dorians, who had thought the area too uninviting to settle. Until the beginning of the sixth century B.C., it was ruled by kings and oligarchs who favored a small group of rich landowners. The conflict between rich and poor grew so dangerous that in 594 B.C. both classes turned for mediation to a merchant named Solon, who had a reputation as a wise counselor. His reforms made enslavement for debts illegal and broke up huge estates held by a few rich landowners. Most important, he drafted a constitution that greatly broadened political power, giving political status to sailors and workmen, and providing for assemblies through which all citizens could participate in the crucial decisions affecting the state. Women, children, alien residents, and slaves were excluded from citizenship. But all free male adults had a direct voice in the government of their city. This privilege, however, carried with it unusual responsibility. All able-bodied citizens between eighteen and sixty years of age were responsible for the defense of the city. During their entire adult lives, all citizens had to take up arms whenever the interests of the city-state called for it.

While democracy was developing in Athens, the Persians were extending their power in the east. By 500 B.C., they had reached the eastern shore of the Aegean. Then, in 490 B.C., Darius, the Persian king, invaded Greece itself, landing at Marathon, outside Athens. The Persians outnumbered the ten thousand Athenians who marched out to meet them by at least two to one, for the Spartans had refused to send troops to aid in the defense of Greece. Without archers or cavalry, the Athenians advanced with their lances lowered right into the Persians, crashing through their lines and driving them back to their ships. Aeschylus fought at Marathon, and his brother died in the battle. Aeschylus considered his participation in the battle more important than his plays, as is revealed in the epitaph he directed to be placed on his tombstone:

> Beneath this stone lies Aeschylus, son of Euphorion, the Athenian. . . . Of his noble prowess the grove of Marathon can speak, or the long-haired Persian who knows it well.

Darius died before he could avenge this humiliating defeat, but in 481 his son Xerxes led another Persian invasion. This time the Spartans saw that all Greece was threatened and joined the Athenians. A band of Spartans led by Leonidas died trying to defend the pass of Thermopylae, but the Persians moved toward Athens, laying waste the countryside as they went. This time they took Athens, destroyed the city, and buried the sacred temples of the Acropolis. But the Athenian navy, commanded by Themistocles, lured the Persian fleet into the narrow Bay of Salamis and crushed it, forcing Xerxes to abandon Athens. What was left of the Persian army was routed by the Spartans at the battle of Plataea a year later. The Persians never again attempted to conquer Greece.

The defeat of the Persians was a milestone in history, not only because it left Greece free to reach the creative heights she achieved in the mid-fifth century, but also because it initiated the decline of Asia and the emergence of Europe as the center of power and progress in the world. The cultural golden age that followed lasted a mere half-century, but in that brief period, Aeschylus, Sophocles, Euripides, Thucydides, Herodotus, Aristophanes, Phidias, Myron, and Socrates all began or finished their amazing contributions to Western civilization.

The symbol of that age is, of course, the Acropolis of Athens, whose ruins stand today as a magnificent monument to the most creative period in history. The man mainly responsible for the environment that produced such creativity was Pericles. Although he was only one of ten generals who formed the executive body that carried out the decisions of the assembly of citizens, he was in his time the most influential man in Greece. He had all the influence of a monarch without any of the power. A man who loved democracy as much as he loved beauty, he chose to command by pure persuasion and he was re-elected to his post every year from 461 to 430 B.C. It was Pericles who persuaded the Athenians to rebuild the Acropolis after it was destroyed by the Persians, and he persuaded them to rebuild it not in wood, as it had been, but in marble. Finally, it was Pericles who marshaled the most brilliant architects and sculptors of the age to accomplish the task. He was so concerned with nourishing the minds and spirits of Athenians that he set aside sixty official holidays a year during which he mounted lavish festivals of drama, dance, and poetry. He even offered to pay the equivalent of a jury-duty fee to those attending dramas, so that even the poorest Athenian could take time off to do so.

As long as Pericles concentrated on artistic achievements, things went well, but he made the mistake of involving Athens in a series of unfortunate imperialist adventures that aroused the jealousy of the Spartans. The result was the Peloponnesian War, which brought the golden age and the glory of Athens to an end. The war began in 431 when the Corinthians, seeing the expansion of Athens as a threat to their trade, appealed to Sparta, which willingly took command of the fight against the Athenians and completely defeated them. The supremacy of the militaristic Spartans was unpopular, not only with Athenians but with other Greeks as well, and it ended in 371 B.C. when the Thebans defeated the Spartan army. During the next few decades,

the continuing rivalry between the Greek city-states provided an opportunity for Philip of Macedon to set about
conquering them. Despite the urgings of Demosthenes, the
Athenian orator who denounced Philip's ambitions in the
four speeches later compiled as the *Philippics*, Athens and
Thebes united too late to stop him. In 339 B.C., he won a
decisive victory against Greek forces that assured the conquest of all Greece. Two years later, Philip was assassinated
and was succeeded by his twenty-year-old son, who would
be known to history as Alexander the Great.

Philip had never intended to end his conquests with
Greece, and in 334 Alexander followed his father's plans
and crossed the Hellespont to crush the Persian empire. He
accomplished that by 327 and pushed on to the Indus River
and what is now Pakistan. He would have continued, but
his armies told him that they had reached their limit, so he
paused to consolidate his rule. When he died of a fever in
325 at thirty-three, practically all the world that Greeks had
ever heard about was his. Alexander's dream of uniting
West and East under one rule died with him. His empire
was divided into three parts: the Asian provinces went to
Seleucus, a general who named a hundred cities after his
father, Antioch. Egypt went to another general, Ptolemy,
who established a dynasty that lasted for three hundred
years (Cleopatra was the last of the Ptolemys). Greece went
to a Macedonian general at first and then to a succession of
warlords. The most notable of these was Pyrrhus, king of
Epirus, who tried to fight the growing power of Rome.
Pyrrhus won a famous battle against Rome on Italian soil
in 279 B.C., but at such great cost that he remarked: "Another victory like this and I am lost."

The period between the death of Alexander and the
Roman conquest is known as the Hellenistic age. Although
the Greek city-states and their democratic governments van-

ished, Greek language and culture prevailed throughout the vast area conquered by Alexander. But it was an inferior culture, for artistic tastes were much less delicate than during the classical period. Sensational effects and striking realism were the rule, and sculpture and drama declined rapidly. However, other disciplines reached new heights. The schools of Plato and Aristotle endured as institutions that nurtured a strong interest in philosophy for centuries. The literary schools of Alexandria in Egypt and Pergamum in Anatolia established grammar as a science and greatly refined literary and artistic criticism. The medical schools expanded man's knowledge of animal anatomy and stimulated research in biology and chemistry. Libraries were established in major cities.

The Romans kept pushing eastward and in 197 B.C. they conquered Macedonia. Fifty years later all of Greece became a Roman province, and for the next four centuries the Romans stole or copied every Greek work of art they laid eyes on. The Romans methodically took over the Greek world, expropriating the artistic and intellectual wealth it offered and making their own contributions in the form of roads, waterworks, and unified administrative and legal systems. The center of the Western world was now Rome, but Greece was still the setting for some of history's most dramatic moments. Julius Caesar fought a decisive battle against Pompey on the plains of Thessaly in 51 B.C. A few years later his nephew, Octavian, defeated the fleet of Marc Antony and Cleopatra on the western coast of Greece near Actium and shattered the dreams of those ambitious lovers. About a century later, Christianity began to spread in Greece. The apostle Paul came to preach the simple faith that was shortly to become the strongest force in the world, and he remained to set up Christian communities in several Greek cities, including Corinth and Athens. In A.D. 325, the emperor Constantine declared Christianity the state religion throughout the empire. Five years later, he established a new capital near the Golden Horn and named it after himself.

Constantinople flourished while Rome was ravaged by successive tribes of barbarians. The empire took the name of the ancient Greek colony on which the capital was built —Byzantium—and survived for a thousand years after the fall of Rome.

In time the language, the culture, even the emperors themselves became Greek. The new Christian thinkers skillfully incorporated Greek philosophical ideas into their ideology, even though the schools of Plato and Aristotle, where the ideas originated, were closed because of their alleged pagan influence. Art and architecture flourished in distinctive new forms that were usually rigid yet strangely moving and beautiful. Byzantine churches, their walls brilliantly decorated with frescoes, mosaics, and icons, are among the most beautiful in Christendom.

One might assume that the emergence of a new Greek culture in Constantinople would have helped Greece to reach new heights, but it did not work out that way. The center of civilization was Constantinople, not Athens, and all the best talents drifted eastward. By the eighth century, when a strong-willed Athenian beauty named Irene became empress, Athens had lost its importance as an intellectual center and had become simply a small provincial town in which the beautiful Parthenon was a Christian church dedicated to the mother of Jesus. Furthermore, because the borders of Greece formed the frontier of the Byzantine empire, the country was periodically ravaged by attacking Slavic tribes. In the eleventh century the Normans, attracted by the wealth of Byzantium, attacked and occupied large sections of Greece. Then, in 1204, the Crusaders, ostensibly

on their way to liberate Jerusalem, captured Constantinople
and held it for more than fifty years. During this period,
Greece was parceled out to Frankish knights who held on
to the land even after the Crusaders relinquished Constantinople.

The Frankish knights tried to Latinize Greece. They im-
planted a feudal system on the Greek social structure, elim-
inated what remained of Roman law, imposed the
supremacy of the Catholic church, and turned Greek trade
over to the Venetians. But in the end the Franks not only
failed to change the land, they wound up being changed by
it. Once more the Greeks held on to their identity and their
religion and slowly conquered their conquerors.

As Nikos Kazantzakis tells it,

> Imperceptibly the feminine landscape began its intimate,
> gentle and noiseless encirclement. The landscape and
> the native women, wheat-brown, black-haired and
> wide-eyed. The blond dragons felt their resistance
> slowly disintegrating. They mingled with the women
> and forgot their homeland. They had children. . . . The
> children emulated their mothers, they spoke the moth-
> er's tongue and became Greeks. The infants' Frankish
> blood retreated. Acrid Greek blood . . . dripped into it,
> and the Frankish blood vanished. A new conquest
> began.

While the Franks were being assimilated in Greece, the
Ottoman Turks were marching relentlessly westward. Constantinople resisted the advance for a time, but on May 29,
1453, it finally collapsed under a massive Ottoman on-
slaught. (The fall of the city occurred on a Tuesday, a day
Greeks have considered highly unlucky ever since. Even
now many Greeks would not think of starting a trip, making an important decision, or taking any action that poses a

significant risk on a Tuesday.) After the fall of Constantinople, the Turks marched on Greece, and by 1460 the
whole country was under their rule. The bondage lasted for
four centuries and left wounds on the Greek spirit that have
yet to heal. To avoid Turkish rule, a number of Greeks fled
to other parts of Europe, where they contributed actively to
the Renaissance. But for the vast majority who stayed behind, life was bleak and brutal. The Turks took over the
best lands and drove the Greeks to barren mountainsides.
They crushed resistance ruthlessly, often capriciously anni-
hilating segments of the male population that might provide
leadership for a rebellion. They picked out the most beautiful Greek girls for their harems, and they took one male
child out of every five for enrollment in the sultan's Janissary Corps. During this brutal subjugation, the Greeks once
again demonstrated their tremendous capacity for survival.
They held on tenaciously to their language, religion, and
culture, and despite numerous setbacks, the dream of freedom burned in their souls for more than four hundred
years. One of the setbacks occurred after the famous battle
of Lepanto in 1571, when a European fleet crushed a Turkish armada in the straits of the Gulf of Corinth. Spurred on
by the victorious Europeans, the Greeks revolted, only to
discover that Turkish power on land had not been affected
by the naval defeat. Turkish troops crushed the rebellion
and slaughtered thousands of Greek revolutionaries.

Greek hopes flickered briefly again late in the seventeenth century when the Venetians, the only Europeans to
hold any Greek territory after the Turkish conquest, used
the islands they controlled as staging points for a drive
against the Turks on the Greek mainland. The Venetians
managed to take Athens briefly, but the only lasting memorial to their stay was the destruction of the Parthenon.
The great temple had survived intact until then, with the

Turks turning it into a mosque. During the siege of Athens, the Turks stored their gunpowder barrels in the Parthenon, and when a Venetian artilleryman scored a hit on the temple with a mortar, it was reduced to the ruin visible today. In 1770 the Greeks rebelled once again, this time encouraged by the Russians posing as champions of Orthodox Christianity. Actually, Russia was then fighting the Ottoman Empire on its own borders and tried to start a second front by sending a force to the Peloponnesus to stir the Greeks to revolt. When Russia's war with the Turks ended, however, Russian forces withdrew from the Peloponnesus, leaving the Greeks on their own. Again the ill-equipped Greek rebels were crushed. Thousands of Greeks, many of whom had not even participated in the revolt, were massacred.

Despite these setbacks, the Greeks grew stronger while the Turks grew weaker. Ironically, the Turks themselves unwittingly helped the Greeks hasten the day when they would throw off their yoke. The Turks looked with disdain both upon trade and administration, and they turned these fields over to the Greeks. In Constantinople there developed a class of powerful Greek administrators and merchants holding some of the most important posts in the Ottoman service. Known as the Phanariots because they lived in a district called the Phanar (Lighthouse), near the residence of the Orthodox patriarch, some of these men grew so powerful that they were able to win concessions from the sultan that helped their fellow Greeks prepare for the struggle to come. One Phanariot, for example, got permission to establish Greek schools in the empire. The schools were important in developing leadership in the Greek communities. In addition, Greeks manned and commanded the trading vessels that brought Turkish goods to European ports. These sailors, responsive as all Greeks to new ideas, reacted to the ferment for change that swept Europe in the wake of the

French Revolution and heightened the desire for Greek independence. When the struggle finally came, the sailors provided an instant navy for the Greek forces. Finally, the Turks made the mistake of putting Orthodox church leaders in charge of their communities. The Turks used the church as an instrument through which to rule, and in so doing, they made priests political as well as spiritual leaders. Those Orthodox priests used their responsibility to keep Greek culture alive in every community and the desire for freedom strong in every generation. The church was not only the vessel for preserving the Orthodox religion: it was also the focal point of the new Greek nationalism. It is not surprising, then, that the revolution that ultimately brought independence to Greece was launched in a church. After an uprising led by a Phanariot named Alexander Ypsilanti erupted in several provinces of what is now Rumania, the Ottoman authorities in the Peloponnesus summoned the primates of the area to the administrative center of Tripolitsa to warn them that any rebellion in Greece would be crushed. Fearful of what awaited them at Tripolitsa, the primates ignored the summons and rushed to the monastery of Aghia Lavra (Saint Laura). There, on March 25, 1821, Archbishop Germanos of Patras blessed the standard of the cross brought by Greek insurgents and started the revolution against the Turks.

The insurrection in the northern provinces, led by Ypsilanti, failed after a few months when the Russians refused to support it. But in the Peloponnesus it took hold. On land, the rising was led by *klephts,* Greek brigands who had taken to the mountains to harass the Turks and who now united to drive them out. On the sea, the great merchant captains who had grown rich carrying Ottoman goods to Europe used their ships and their money to build a Greek navy. In two years, the two groups almost succeeded in clearing both the land and the sea of Turks. (Both groups produced military leaders whom modern Greeks consider heroes on a par with Leonidas and Themistocles. On land they included Theodoros Kolokotronis and George Karaiskakis, and on the sea Andreas Miaoulis and Constantine Kanaris.)

With independence in sight, however, the generals and the admirals began to bicker about who would command the most power after the war was won. The Turks took advantage of this dissension and with the aid of the European-trained forces of the Ottoman commander Mehemet Ali, the pasha of Egypt, nullified the effect of nearly all the Greek victories. By the end of 1822, a large segment of the Greek land forces was bottled up at Missolonghi, a small seaport on the northern shore of the Gulf of Corinth. During the subsequent siege of the town, Lord Byron, who had gone to Greece along with other philhellenes from Europe

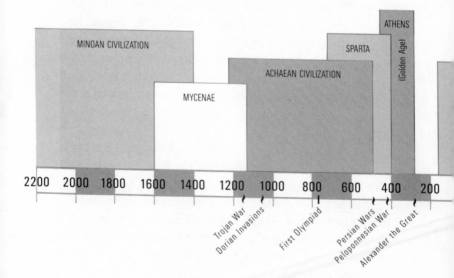

Approximate time-chart of Greek history, showing the main per

and the United States to fight on the side of the insurgents, died of a fever. Missolonghi fell after a heroic defense that aroused the admiration of all Europe. Seeing that the end was near, the defenders set fire to the ammunition stores and blew themselves and a good number of their attackers to pieces.

The Turks massacred thousands of people as they reconquered liberated areas one by one. They even hanged the Patriarch of Constantinople, the spiritual leader of all Orthodox Christians, which offended the sensibilities of people everywhere, particularly after such artists as Delacroix began to depict it on canvas. It also touched the self-interest of the great European powers. England and France feared that Russia, an Orthodox country, would use the massacre of Orthodox Christians in Greece to enter the war and win a foothold in the Mediterranean. To prevent such a move, England and France sent emissaries to Moscow and

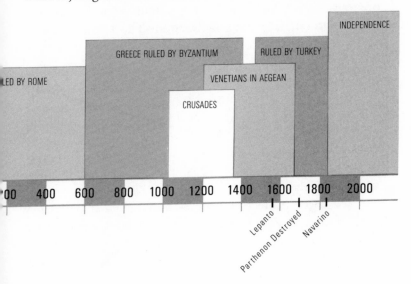

uences, and some of the events mentioned in this book.

told the czar that they would join Russia in urging Turkey to grant the Greeks some degree of independence.

In the summer of 1827, the three powers, serving as self-appointed mediators, proclaimed an armistice. The Greeks accepted it but the Turks did not, so the Allies sent a force of ships to the scene of hostilities. The Allied fleet met the combined Turkish and Egyptian armada at the Battle of Navarino in Pylos Bay off the southwestern coast of the Peloponnesus on October 20, 1827. Although outnumbered, the Allies had vastly superior firepower and sent sixty enemy ships to the bottom without losing a single one of their own. Within a year, Mehemet Ali signed an agreement with England and France providing for a complete withdrawal of Egyptian troops from the Peloponnesus. Russia then launched a war of its own against the Turks and forced the sultan to accept the loss of part of Greece to end it. Fearing that the Russian victory would give the czar a preponderant influence in Greece, England and France conferred with the Russians in London. The resulting agreement declared Greece an independent state but limited its territory for the most part to the Peloponnesus, Attica, and the Cyclade islands. This was an area much smaller than anything previously discussed by the three powers for the new country. The idea was that if Greece was kept small its influence in the Mediterranean would be limited and the three powers would be less likely to fight over it. The agreement also called for the establishment of a hereditary monarchy in Greece.

The three protecting powers had agreed that the new king of Greece would not come from their own ruling families, so the choice fell on the seventeen-year-old Bavarian Prince Otto. He arrived in his ready-made kingdom on February 6, 1833, but his reign was autocratic, unpopular, and ineffectual. In 1862, while on a tour of the provinces, he learned that a revolt against him had erupted in Athens, and in one of his few moments of wisdom, he took his wife and boarded the nearest ship sailing out of Greece.

With Otto gone, the protecting powers looked around for another instrument through whom to maintain their hold on Greek affairs. They settled on Prince William of Denmark, who came to the throne as George I. He ruled for half a century, from 1863 to 1913, and proved to be much more astute than the inflexible Otto. During his reign, and with the aid of able political leaders, notably Kharalios Trikoupis, Greece took major strides toward assuming a proper place in the European family of nations. Trikoupis held the realistic view that free Greece should be developed into a strong nation before efforts were made to enlarge its territory. He was vindicated in 1881 when, after years of persistent coaxing, Greece succeeded in persuading the Great Powers to make Turkey cede Thessaly and a corner of Epirus to Greece.

Trikoupis became prime minister in 1883 and for the next twelve years built the strong political and economic foundations necessary to carry Greece into the twentieth century. But after his death, in 1906, his successor, Theodore Deliyiannis, was moved by an insurrection in Crete to declare war on the Ottoman Empire. Greece was defeated in a brief and humiliating campaign. The protecting powers intervened and forced Turkish troops to leave Crete, but the island remained under the suzerainty of the sultan.

At the turn of the century, a series of events occurred that set the stage for a new order in Greece dominated by Eleutherios Venizelos, a brilliant politician from Crete. The middle class became thoroughly dissatisfied with the limited progress the country was making under the leadership of a favored oligarchy unwilling to share political power. And all Greeks became impatient with the failure of Greek diplomacy to deal with the threat posed by the Young Turks, who seized power from the sultan in 1908, and who were trying to restore Turkish military authority in the Mediterranean. In 1909, a league of young Greek officers demanded immediate political reforms and a complete reorganization of the armed forces. The ensuing crisis was ultimately resolved when all parties agreed to call Venizelos to form a new government. His talents as the political leader of Greeks in Crete had already earned him a wide reputation. Within months of his arrival in 1910, Venizelos launched reforms that dramatically changed all sectors of life in Greece, from education to agriculture and jurisprudence.

But Venizelos's greatest achievements were diplomatic as he pursued what was called the Great Idea—the political union of all Greeks in the Mediterranean. In 1912, Venizelos formed an alliance with Montenegro, Serbia, and Bulgaria—the Balkan League—against the Ottoman Empire. In October of that year, the League forced the Turks into the first of the two so-called Balkan Wars and inflicted a series of such quick and stunning defeats that the European powers intervened. Under the settlement of 1913, Greece was given Crete and parts of Epirus and Macedonia. But the European powers insisted on the creation of an independent Albania out of territory claimed by Serbia and Greece to keep those ambitious new states from spreading too far. The Greeks, therefore, were denied the long-sought territory of northern Epirus, a loss to which they have yet to reconcile themselves. Greece and Serbia accepted the treaty, but Bulgaria felt that her two allies had gotten more out of the settlement than she had, so she declared war on them, claiming most of Macedonia as her own. Bulgaria was quickly defeated, however, and the border of Macedonia was fixed to Greece's satisfaction. Venizelos had doubled the territory and the population of Greece in less than three

years: a good part of Macedonia, half of Epirus, all of
Crete, and most of the Aegean islands became a permanent
part of Greece—a gain of 17,000 square miles and 1.7 million
people.

When World War I broke out in 1914, Venizelos
wanted to commit Greece immediately on the side of the
Allies. With the Ottoman Empire and Bulgaria committed
to the Central Powers, Venizelos reasoned that an Allied
victory would give Greece a tremendous opportunity to ac-
quire territory from the Powers and so help to fulfill the
Great Idea. Constantine I, who had succeeded when his
father George I was assassinated in 1913, had other plans.
Educated in Germany and married to a sister of Kaiser Wilhelm, Constantine wanted Greece to support the Central
Powers, and he resisted Venizelos so strongly that he forced
him to resign in 1915. The country was hopelessly divided
for the next two years until the Allies forced Constantine to
abdicate in favor of his son, Alexander, and Venizelos was
recalled as prime minister. In the autumn of 1918, when the
Allies marched toward Constantinople, the Greek army was
in the vanguard, and by the end of the year Bulgaria had
surrendered and Turkey had agreed to an armistice. In various treaties, Greece got western Thrace from Bulgaria and
eastern Thrace from the Turks.

Most significantly, Venizelos presented his case so
forcefully at the Versailles peace talks that he won the Allies' permission to occupy Smyrna in May 1919. At that
time, 20 percent of all Greeks still lived under Ottoman rule
in Asia Minor and, from his foothold in Smyrna, Venizelos
hoped to bring under Greek rule the vast Turkish areas that
were once part of the Byzantine empire. The presence of
Greek troops in Asia Minor solidified Turkish resistance,
however, and under their leader, Mustafa Kemal, later
known as Atatürk, they were able to confront the Greeks

on both military and diplomatic fronts, and ultimately isolate them from their allies.

In October 1920, Venizelos, unwisely encouraged by the British Prime Minister Lloyd George, ordered the Greek force to advance against Kemal's still unorganized army. On October 25, the young King Alexander died from the bite of a pet monkey. In a general election in November, Venizelos was rejected by the war-weary Greeks who, in December, voted in a plebiscite to recall Constantine as king. The Greek troops pushed deeper and deeper into the bleak Anatolian interior. When they were weak and exhausted, Kemal attacked; in the retreat, 50,000 Greeks were killed. After they drove the Greek army into the sea at Smyrna, the Turks turned on the Greek settlers in Anatolia, subjugating them to rape, arson, and indiscriminate slaughter.

Again Constantine was forced to abdicate, this time in favor of his second son, George II; again the country turned to Venizelos. For several months, he negotiated with Turkish emissaries in Switzerland and finally secured a peace agreement that entailed the greatest exchange of populations in the Mediterranean: 400,000 Turks in Greece for 1,250,000 Greeks in Turkey. (Among them was a sixteen-year-old tobacco merchant's son named Aristotle Onassis.) The Greeks left vast holdings in Asia Minor and, taking practically nothing but the clothes on their backs, they had to resettle in a land hard-pressed to feed the people already living in it. But everyone realized that the Greeks overseas could not have been left at the mercy of the Turks, and Venizelos once again won the support of his countrymen for his decisive statesmanship.

He not only secured the safety of Greeks in Asia Minor, but won a border with the Turks in Thrace that was much more favorable than anyone had dared to hope. When he returned from Switzerland Venizelos could have made himself ruler of Greece for life. Instead he tried to build strong democratic institutions in the country where they were first conceived. He did not succeed, primarily because of the opposition of reactionary forces and the impatience of his own supporters. In 1923, George II was forced into exile and a republic was established that lasted twelve years. During this period, Venizelos was in and out of office eight times as his supporters fought as fiercely among themselves as with the royalist opposition. In November 1935, George was recalled from exile, and two months later elections were held that split royalists and republicans practically down the middle and gave the balance of power to fifteen Communist deputies. The king, therefore, asked General Ioannis Metaxas to form a new government. Metaxas, a man in tune with the Fascist mood of Europe at the time, did form a government briefly, then dissolved Parliament and began to rule by decree. Shortly afterward, Venizelos died in exile in Paris and his body was shipped directly to Crete for burial because the new dictator feared the consequences if he allowed it to lie in state in Athens.

Metaxas ruled for almost five years, leavening his repressive measures with enough social reforms to allow Greeks to justify his existence, and, in the end, proved to be a patriot, despite his fondness for Fascism. On October 28, 1940, the Italian ambassador drove to Metaxas's home and presented him with an ultimatum from Mussolini demanding that Greek borders be opened immediately to Italian troops. Metaxas, speaking to the ambassador in French, rejected the ultimatum with the words, *"Alors, c'est la guerre!"* But popular legend has condensed Metaxas's refusal into the single word, *"Ochi!"* ("No!"), which has become a battle cry that blooms defiantly every October 28—Ochi Day—on walls throughout Greece. As recounted in

Chapter 1, the Italians met ignominious defeat, and Hitler, in order to prevent an Axis debacle in Greece, sent in crack SS troops, tanks, and Stuka bombers in the spring of 1941. The Greeks see their defeat of the Italians as playing a key role in the ultimate Allied victory over the Germans.

During the terrible years of the occupation, many thousands of Greeks were either executed by the Germans or allowed to die of starvation. Nevertheless, of all the peoples conquered by the Nazis, none fought back harder than the Greeks. Sadly, however, the resistance fighters battled each other with almost as much fury as they did the Nazis. Two main groups were involved—the National Liberation Front (EAM), whose military arm was called the National Popular Liberation Army (ELAS), and the pro-Western, conservative Greek Democratic League (EDES). The EAM-ELAS group consisted at first of a broad coalition of liberals, Socialists, and Communists, but later it became almost completely dominated by the better-organized Communists. By 1944, when the Germans withdrew from Greece, EAM-ELAS was a much larger and stronger force than EDES. In firm control of two-thirds of the country, it launched a brutal purge of "collaborators," a label it applied to anyone opposed to communism. To prevent the Communists from consolidating their hold, Winston Chruchill dispatched British troops to Greece. The Greek Communists hardly welcomed the British intervention, but they submitted to it under pressure from Stalin, who had agreed that Greece should fall in the British sphere of influence in return for Poland's falling in the Soviet sphere.

When the British called for all guerrilla forces to disband, EAM-ELAS resisted and conducted a protest rally in Constitution Square, Athens. Right-wing police fired on the unarmed demonstrators and the bloody Battle of Athens began. It lasted thirty-three days and took the lives of

13,500 people. The struggle brought Churchill himself to Athens to arrange a truce. On February 12, 1945, representatives of EAM-ELAS and the provisional Greek government led by Premier George Papandreou met the British ambassador in Varkiza, a seaside town near Athens, and signed an agreement calling for liberal reforms, the recognition of a Communist party, a plebiscite on the monarchy, and elections within a year. By the time elections were actually held in March, 1946, however, the leaders of the Greek Communist Party (KKE), having missed the opportunity to seize power at the end of the occupation and later during the Battle of Athens, decided to set the stage for another attempt, which they called "the third round." They ordered their followers and sympathizers to abstain from the voting so that a right-wing government would be elected and the country would be polarized. Unfortunately, that is exactly what happened: a right-wing government was elected and General Zervas of EDES was appointed minister of public order. The new regime answered Communist force with force, and the mountains began to fill with guerrillas. When the plebiscite on the return of the king was held in September, Greece was on the brink of civil war, and many liberals voted with the royalists in the hope that the return of the king would result in the creation of a stable and responsible political climate.

It was too late. Civil war broke out and the KKE ordered its guerrillas to stop at nothing to conquer the country. Within a few months considerable areas of northern Greece and the Peloponnesus were under Communist control and the rest of the country was on the brink of economic collapse. Unable to cope, the British asked the United States to intervene. President Truman responded firmly and quickly. A U.S. economic mission was sent to Greece and given a major voice in the Greek government, which began to moderate its excessive policies and to win the support of the people. A U.S. military mission under General James Van Fleet helped the Greek army reorganize into an effective force and relocated 700,000 mountain villagers to choke off the supply of men used by the guerrillas. Unable to expand their territory or to augment their forces, the frustrated Communists, led by party leader Nikos Zachariadis and military commander Markos Vafiades, tried ruthlessly to hold on to what they had. They drafted girls into their fighting units, abducted some 28,000 children from their parents and sent them to indoctrination camps in Eastern Europe, and executed thousands of men, women, and young people in order to frighten the rest into total obedience (my mother was one of the victims). The terror, however, only succeeded in alienating many who had originally favored the Communists both in and out of Greece, and when Marshal Tito closed the Yugoslav border to the guerrillas after breaking with Stalin in 1948, the tide turned irrevocably against them. After a last, bloody stand on the mountains of Vitsi and Grammos in northern Greece, the guerrillas abandoned the struggle in 1949. Taking captives as they went, they retreated behind the Iron Curtain.

U.S. aid under the Truman Doctrine not only helped to save Greece from the Communists, but also helped to rebuild it after almost ten years of war and devastation. During the reconstruction period, three groups struggled to hold political power. The extreme left united under the Communist-front party called EDA (Union of the Democratic Left), but managed to pull only about 15 percent of the vote in most elections. The liberals, chiefly shopkeepers and skilled workers, were split between several parties. Power, therefore, fell to the conservatives, who in the period after the civil war were led by Field Marshal Alexander Papagos, the commander of Greek forces against the Communists.

Papagos died in 1955 and was succeeded by Constantine Karamanlis, who kept the conservative party, the National Radical Union (ERE), in power for eight years. A tough, able leader, Karamanlis worked hard to build up the economy of Greece and give the country stable government. By 1960 the Greek economy was growing at the impressive rate of 8 percent a year. In the 1961 elections, Karamanlis's party was strongly challenged by the Center Union, a coalition of several liberal parties now united under a single banner and headed by George Papandreou, who had led the first postwar Greek government. In fact, the Center Union claimed that the winning margin had been the result of coercion and fraud in the rural areas, where the army and gendarmerie had considerable arbitrary authority. As Karamanlis's popularity continued to decline, he began to lose the support of the palace as well, and in 1963 he resigned. The election that followed brought George Papandreou's Center Union to power, but with so small a majority that it needed the support of the Communist-front party in Parliament. Papandreou refused Communist backing and resigned at the end of 1963, calling for new elections. This time the Center Union won by 53 percent of the vote—the largest plurality in postwar Greek history. King Paul died a month after the election and was succeeded by his son, Constantine II. The young king clashed with the prime minister over control of the armed forces, and dismissed Papandreou in 1965. Constantine formed a new government with dissenters from Papandreou's party, but it remained shaky. Parliament was dissolved and new elections were called. They never took place.

A week after the dissolution of Parliament, on April 21, 1967, Greek army units led by a group of colonels seized power in a predawn coup. The junta, headed by Colonel George Papadopoulos, suspended individual rights, prohibited all political activity, imposed harsh restrictions on the

press, and arrested thousands of people. The king remained
nominal head of state but deprived of power. At the end of
the year he tried to overthrow the colonels but failed and
fled with his family to Italy. Papadopoulos appointed himself prime minister. In an effort to win public support, he
released some political prisoners, increased workers' pen-
sions, and canceled bank debts of Greek farmers. In 1973,
Papadopoulos abolished the monarchy after a mutiny of
royalist naval officers. He proclaimed the country a republic
and named himself provisional president. After he announced plans for a limited return to parliamentary rule,
hard-liners in the army used a student revolt in Athens in
November to oust him and reimpose tight military control.
The new junta used Greek officers in Cyprus to overthrow
the government of Archbishop Makarios, who refused to
bend to the will of the colonels. In 1974, Turkey accused
Greece of violating Cypriot independence and invaded the
island. After several days of fighting, a cease-fire was signed
to prevent full-scale war between Greece and Turkey, osten-
sible allies who formed the southern flank of NATO.
Backed by 30,000 troops, Turkish Cypriots took possession
of one-third of the island, although they represented only
18 percent of the population.

The Cyprus debacle made the position of the military
rulers in Athens untenable, and they invited Constantine
Karamanlis, who had been living in Paris since 1963, to
return and form a civilian government. After establishing
himself as prime minister, Karamanlis put the junta leaders
on trial for treason: the 1967 coup. They were found guilty
and sentenced to life in prison in October. A month later,
the first free elections in a decade were held and were won
by the New Democracy Party led by Karamanlis, who then
called for a plebiscite on the monarchy. Karamanlis refused
to declare himself on the issue, and Greeks voted two to
one for a republic.

Over the next five years, Karamanlis made a special effort to take Greece into the Common Market, an effort that bore fruit with the signing of the Treaty of Accession in Athens on May 23, 1979. A year later, Karamanlis resigned as prime minister and was elected president by Parliament.

By then the New Democracy Party he founded was facing strong pressure from the main opposition party, the Panhellenic Socialist Movement (PASOK), which won a parliamentary majority in the 1981 elections under the leadership of Andreas Papandreou, son of former Prime Minster George Papandreou. PASOK came to power on a platform that attacked Greece's strong ties with the West, and charged that the country's Western allies, and particularly the Americans, had repeatedly betrayed Greece in favor of its rival, Turkey. As prime minister, Papandreou often sided with the Soviet Union on international issues rather than with the United States, where he had lived for twenty years, although he did not carry out his campaign threats to throw out U.S. bases and to pull Greece out of NATO and the Common Market.

The year 1985 brought both parliamentary elections for president and national elections for a new government. PASOK support was needed to re-elect Karamanlis president, and Papandreou repeatedly stated he would provide it. But shortly before Parliament voted, Papandreou changed his mind, refused to back Karamanlis, and put in his own man instead. In the national elections that followed, Papandreou's party again prevailed, but his new government was quickly forced to impose austerity measures to try to revive a troubled economy of rising unemployment and inflation, declining productivity, and soaring foreign debt.

Many Greeks have tended to blame their country's problems in the past on meddling kings or foreign powers.

With the monarchy gone after the 1974 plebiscite and all the levers of government controlled by men who opposed ties to the West after the ouster of Karamanlis, the restraints they had found so onerous were gone. After 1985, Greeks were completely on their own and without excuses, feeling perhaps a little like the citizens described by their renowned poet, C. P. Cavafy:

> And now what will become of us
>   without Barbarians?—
> Those people were some sort of a solution.

SIX

God
and
Man

"We preserve the Doctrine of the Lord
uncorrupted . . . neither adding any thing,
nor taking any thing from it."
LETTER OF THE ORTHODOX PATRIARCHS,
1718

In Greece, the church permeates every layer of life.
A Greek's year is based on the festivals of the
church calendar. He is feted not on his birthday but on the
day of the saint for which he was named. Greeks who have
moved to the cities will return to their home town on the
feast day of the local saint to participate in the services,
picnic, and festivities. When any endeavor, such as the
building of a new house, is begun, the priest is asked to say
a blessing on the spot. The local church is not a place to
visit only on Sundays. Whenever a Greek has a problem, he
will light a candle to the saint most likely to hear his prayers
and intercede in the matter. He may even buy a small flat
metal (possibly silver or gold) image of what is causing him
concern: ship, baby, woman, man, arm, leg, eye, house, and
place the token before the icon. Old and venerated icons
show that pilgrims have been asking for intercession for
hundreds of years—some of the tiny metal figures hung on
them wear clothes in old Turkish and even medieval styles.
Every event of the year—the sowing of crops, the first voy-
age of the village fishing fleet, the first fruits of the harvest

—is marked with an appropriate religious ceremony. Pilgrimages are often made to especially holy shrines. On the island of Tenos, in 1823, an icon of the Virgin was discovered buried under a ruined church. This icon is believed to have miraculous healing powers and to effect several cures a year. The sick make pilgrimages to Tenos just as Roman Catholics travel to Lourdes. The greatest crowds arrive on the Feast of the Assumption, August 15, and spend the night jammed together inside the church and in the streets around it.

It is not surprising that religion is so important in Greece. During the hundreds of years when the Turks ruled the country, only their church provided Greeks with a sense of unity and national identity. The music, art, literature, and oral history that survived the Turkish occupation were conserved by the churches and monasteries. Greece is the only country in the world that is still officially Orthodox. The Orthodox faith, the third largest branch of Christianity, has about 150 million followers, including the 10 million within Greece and many more Greeks outside the country. Orthodoxy is often described as being very close to Roman Catholicism in doctrine, but close to Protestantism in feeling.

The date usually assigned to the split between the Eastern and Western branches of the church is 1054, when the Pope excommunicated the Patriarch of Constantinople and the Patriarch in turn excommunicated the Pope. In liturgy and outlook the Orthodox church is most similar to the primitive Christian church, and in many ways it has remained remarkably unchanged over the centuries. Because Orthodoxy has so often existed under rulers of alien faiths —Arabs, Turks, Mongols—surviving churches became ghettos of conservatism, fighting to preserve the old faith rather than permitting it to change and evolve.

Among the things that the Orthodox share with Roman Catholics are: belief in both church tradition and Scripture as the source of revelation, the seven sacraments instituted by Christ, the doctrine of the Trinity formulated by the first seven General Councils before 800, and devotion to the Virgin Mary and to the saints.

To understand what the Greeks believe and how their church is structured, it is necessary to go back into Christian history. When, in A.D. 313, the Roman emperor Constantine was converted to Christianity by a vision of a cross in the sky, Roman persecution of the church ended. It became an officially tolerated religion and then, some years after Constantine's death, the only recognized religion of the Roman empire. Constantine took several steps that were to prove momentous for Christianity. In 324, he decided to move the capital of the empire to the site of a Greek city on the Bosporus called Byzantium. There, on a magnificent location at the gateway between Europe and Asia, he built the "New Rome," which he named Constantinople in honor of himself. He also convoked the Council of Nicaea, the first of seven great General Councils that clarified and articulated the organization of the church and defined its teachings on the doctrines of the Trinity and the Incarnation. The Council of Nicaea singled out patriarchs as holding a position of special seniority: the bishops of Rome, Alexandria, and Antioch. Later councils added the bishops of Constantinople and Jerusalem. At the fourth General Council, an order of precedence was established for the five great sees of the church: Rome first, then Constantinople, Alexandria, Antioch, and Jerusalem. All five claimed to have been founded by the Apostles. The five patriarchs divided among themselves the religious jurisdiction over the whole known world (except for Cyprus, which was self-governing). However, in the case of a doctrinal dispute, the

patriarchs alone could not meet to settle it; every bishop of
the church had an equal right to speak and to vote at a
General Council (and in the Orthodox faith still has). The
Pope was given a primacy of honor because St. Peter and
St. Paul were martyred in Rome and because Rome was the
chief city of the ancient world. He was not, however, given
primacy of jurisdiction, but merely considered the first
among equals.

The seventh and last General Council was held in 787.
Thereafter a schism between Rome and the patriarchates of
the East slowly began to develop. The final break was a
result of many factors: cultural, political, economic, and
theological. Originally the church had been held together
by the political and cultural unity of the Roman empire.
Educated men spoke both Greek and Latin. But from the
fifth century on, barbarian invasions fractured the unity of
the Mediterranean world. With the rise of Islam, the Mediterranean Sea fell mainly under Arab control and the West
was cut off from Byzantium. In 800, the Pope crowned one
of the "barbarians"—Charles the Great, King of the Franks
—in Rome and made him Emperor Charlemagne. By that
time, most scholars in the West understood only Latin while
those in the East read only Greek.

Eventually two differences in doctrine became crucial.
The Pope held that he was infallible and had powers of
jurisdiction over all the church, East and West, while the
Greek church held that in matters of faith a council representing all the bishops must make decisions (although the
Pope was considered to have the right to the most honor-
able seat at such a council). The second great doctrinal
difficulty concerned the ancient Nicene-Constantinopolitan
Creed, which was repeated in all Christian churches. The
original wording stated that the Holy Spirit proceeds "from
the Father" and the Orthodox church still recites it this

way. But the Western church added the word *filioque*, thus saying that the Spirit proceeded "from the Father *and the Son.*" This insertion became a bone of contention that persists today. The Orthodox cite as the basis of their belief John 15:26, in which Christ says, "When the Comforter has come, whom I will send to you from the Father—the Spirit of Truth, who *proceeds from the Father*—he will bear witness to me."

There were other, less inflammatory differences between the two branches of the church: the East allowed priests to marry, the West did not; the rules of fasting varied between East and West; and the Eastern church used leavened bread in the Eucharist, while in the West unleavened bread was used.

The estrangement was displayed in several ways. A patriarch of Constantinople neglected to include the Pope's name on a list of the patriarchs of the church. The Normans, in Byzantine Italy, forced the churches there to conform to Western customs. In retaliation, the Patriarch of Constantinople closed Latin churches in Constantinople. In 1054 both sides made an effort to resolve their differences. Pope Leo sent emissaries to Constantinople, but the meeting became so unfriendly that the papal legate finally walked into the Church of the Holy Wisdom (Hagia, or Saint, Sophia), the most sacred cathedral of the Eastern empire, placed a Bull of Excommunication on the altar, and marched out, saying, "Let God look and judge."

For many years most people of the East and the West were unaware of the great schism between them. But the Crusaders brought the point home to the ordinary Christian with devastating impact. After capturing Antioch from the Turks, the Crusaders set up their own Latin patriarch to rival the Greek patriarch already there. Then, in 1204, the Crusaders temporarily abandoned their drive on Egypt and

sacked the city of Constantinople, desecrating St. Sophia
and tearing its altar and icons to pieces. In the words of one
Orthodox Christian of the period, "Even the Saracens are
merciful and kind compared with these men who bear the
Cross of Christ on their shoulders."

After 1204, the two churches grew farther apart. The
West entered a great period of scholasticism, a major development of the understanding of Christian doctrine in terms
of Aristotelian philosophy. The East, in contrast, carefully
preserved the doctrinal understanding of the fourth-century
church fathers. The Eastern church received a strong infu-
sion of mysticism during the fourteenth century. Some Orthodox believers had long practiced the constant repetition
of the "Jesus prayer": "Lord Jesus Christ, Son of God, have
mercy on me, a sinner," while doing certain physical and
breathing exercises in order to help their concentration.
They believed that after a while it was possible for the Jesus
prayer to "enter the heart" so that it recited itself sponta-
neously, constantly, no matter what the believer was doing,
and whether he was asleep or awake. Their goal was to
attain the mystical experience of seeing the vision of "divine
and uncreated light." These believers were called Hesy-
chasts (the word means one who is silent). They were suc-
cessfully defended by Saint Gregory Palamas, and in the
fourteenth century two Orthodox councils upheld the He-
sychast beliefs. Ever since, the Jesus prayer has played an
important part in the devotions of the Orthodox.

The threatening Ottoman advance led the Byzantine
church into several abortive attempts to reunite with the
Western church. These efforts were very unpopular and
were never accepted by the Orthodox laity. Finally, in 1453,
the Turks attacked Constantinople, killed the emperor,
took the city, and turned St. Sophia into a mosque. The
Byzantine empire had come to an end.

The victorious Moslems allowed the Christians to continue to practice their religion, but they were forced to pay
heavy taxes and were forbidden to serve in the army or to
marry Moslems. To convert a Moslem to Christianity was
a crime punishable by death. Although separation of church
and secular power had been one of the tenets of the Orthodox church, the Moslems forced the Orthodox Patriarch of
Constantinople to become the political head of all Christians under Ottoman rule, thus making him the secular head
of the Greek nation. This semi-tolerance of the Christians
proved far more disabling in the long run than outright
persecution would have been. The ecclesiastical power was
hopelessly intertwined with secular power. Only the sultan
could appoint church leaders, and he was susceptible to
bribery. Thus, the higher administration of the church fell
prey to corruption, ambition, and intrigue.

After the Ottoman empire began to shrink in the nineteenth century, the Orthodox churches of various nations
liberated from Turkish domination threw off the rule of the
Patriarch of Constantinople as well and became the independent churches of Greece, Rumania, Bulgaria, and Serbia.
Today the Orthodox church is composed of fifteen self-
governing or "autocephalous" churches and three churches
that are termed "autonomous" but that have not yet attained full self-government. The autonomous churches are
Finland, Japan, and Macedonia. The autocephalous
churches are the four ancient patriarchates—Constantinople, Alexandria, Antioch, and Jerusalem—plus Russia,
Rumania, Serbia, Bulgaria, Georgia, Cyprus, Czechoslovakia, Poland, Albania, Sinai, and Greece. Perhaps 85 percent of the Orthodox church is now behind the Iron
Curtain.

To attempt to define a church's doctrine in a few pages
is a dangerous undertaking, but I would like to mention

some facets of the Orthodox religion that have significant bearing on life in Greece. Monasticism plays a distinctive and important part in the Orthodox church. Even before Christ, the life of hermits who lived outside civilization had many precedents in Hellenistic and Jewish religions. During the fourth century, a wave of asceticism prompted more and more Christians to move into caves and tombs and even into the desert, the better to devote themselves to their principal task of struggling with devils. Some hermits formed small groups that often revered one monk as their spiritual leader. Such communities gradually evolved into primitive monasteries. In the fourth century, Basil the Great wrote treatises on asceticism that are the basis of the community life of Orthodox monks today.

Orthodox monasteries, unlike some Roman Catholic monasteries, are devoted chiefly to asceticism and mysticism, and only to a limited degree to teaching, missionary efforts, social work, and other activities. Moreover, most Orthodox monks are not clerics but laymen. Just as in the primitive church, there are no separate orders: all monks wear the same habit, follow the same liturgy, and have the same goal—through meditation and prayer to free themselves from the temptations of this world and to achieve a union with Christ. Although there are no separate orders, there are three kinds of Orthodox monks. The majority live in a community under the direction of an abbot and share services, meals, work, and all property. They are cenobitic monks. In some monasteries, however, the monks live in special separate rooms or in small settlements of two or three within a loosely knit community and come together only on Sundays and feast days. These are the Idiorrhythmic monks—living according to their own rhythm. The third category is composed of the anchorites, who live like hermits, usually in inaccessible places, and never see anyone.

Often the anchorite's only contact with civilization is a rope by which he hauls supplies up to his precarious perch.

All three kinds of monks are still active today in Greece, especially in the unique area of Mt. Athos, the Holy Mountain (*Aghion Oros*); even before Christianity, Mt. Athos was referred to as the Peak of God. Here, on this steep, rocky promontory in Macedonia that projects eastward into the Aegean Sea, about fifteen hundred monks live in monasteries, settlements, and caves. Life has scarcely changed in centuries. The day passes in prayer and meditation (in some monasteries the daily recitation of the Divine Office can take ten hours or more).

Athos is an autonomous republic within the Greek state; it includes Russian, Serbian, Bulgarian, and Romanian as well as Greek communities. Certain of the hermits on the mountain are considered living saints, but some observers fear that the monastic life on Athos is doomed because so much of the Orthodox church is behind the Iron Curtain and the number of monks has declined from some twenty thousand to the present figure. Others argue that monks have lived on the mountain continuously for more than a thousand years and that at times there have been even fewer than there are now. In the past fifteen years, there has been a fresh influx of young Greeks, and so once more in many of the monasteries of Athos the spiritual life of classic Orthodoxy remains as vital as it was in the earliest days of Christianity.

Icons play a central part in the Orthodox religion. The word in Greek means image. The interior of every Orthodox church is magnificently adorned with icons and in most Orthodox homes some of these paintings of holy figures may be found hanging. A worshiper, upon entering church, goes up to the iconostasis—a wall of icons that separates the sanctuary from the nave—and kisses the icon of Christ, then of the Blessed Virgin Mary, then those of the saints and angels. Each icon has its ordained place inside the church. Ancient and venerated icons are often nearly completely covered in precious metals and sometimes studded with gems to protect them from the lips of the worshipers. Only the faces of the saints are left uncovered.

During the eighth and ninth centuries, the Byzantine church was rocked by a passionate debate between iconoclasts—those who would do away with icons—and those who defended them as essential to the faith. In the end, the veneration of icons was upheld, and the church sets aside a day every year to honor this victory. But while these two-dimensional images are essential to Orthodox worship, three-dimensional images are strictly forbidden. Icons are stylized images of holy figures and saints, usually painted on wood, but also done in mosaic or enamel work. The gaunt, elongated figures in stylized poses are portrayed in vivid colors against a gold background representing a heavenly aura. The painting of icons has varied so little through the centuries that sometimes only a few experts can tell in which century an icon was made. In the Orthodox church, it is essential that every icon of a holy figure resemble as closely as possible every previous image of that figure. The Orthodox believe that an icon is a kind of window between earth and heaven through which the inhabitants of heaven have chosen to reveal themselves. There are many legends of icons that miraculously appeared, "not made by hands" (*acheiropoietoi*). A supernatural light reportedly emanates from these icons for some time. Other images, especially of Christ, are believed to have been painted by the apostle Luke. The making of an icon is a holy task, and monks fast, do penances, and consecrate their brushes, paints, and pieces of wood before they begin. Sometimes each monk does only one part of each icon, such as the eyes, and then passes it on to another monk. These images form part of holy tradition so that the slightest variation might involve doctrinal distortion or even heresy.

The Orthodox consider icons to be sacred images of holy archetypes—a neoplatonic concept that has many levels of complexity. The apostles, saints, martyrs, prophets, and sacred beings shown in the icons represent the congregation of heaven. The Orthodox believe that during the Eucharist, Christ and the entire heavenly congregation literally manifest themselves and are present, in a foretaste of the second coming. The many icons that deck the church represent the heavenly congregation, and their rich beauty represents the beauty of the divine liturgy in heaven. God himself is considered to be the first iconographer because he portrayed himself through the incarnation in the flesh of Jesus Christ. It is also believed that Christ made the first Christ icon. According to an ancient legend, he sent to King Abgar of Edessa a cloth with which he had dried his face and on the cloth his portrait appeared. The saints are regarded as themselves being images or icons of Christ, and to venerate them is to venerate their archetype, Christ. Every man, as well, is an image of God—no matter how imperfect. Thus, every one of us carries the icon of God within ourselves. These beliefs, central to Orthodoxy, lead to a much greater emphasis on man's nobility and much less emphasis on original sin than is found in Roman Catholicism.

Easter (reckoned according to slightly different rules from those in the West) is the central holiday in the Orthodox faith, and the emphasis is not on the Crucifixion but the Resurrection. As Timothy Ware, Fellow of Pembroke College, Oxford, and the first Englishman to become a bishop in the Greek Orthodox Church, writes in his book, *The Orthodox Church*, "Calvary is seen always in the light of the empty tomb; the Cross is an emblem of victory." Throughout Orthodoxy runs a strong current of rejoicing and jubilation (*chara*) that characterized the early Christian church, whose members joyously anticipated the Second Coming and their participation in the Kingdom of God. Mourning, sorrow, and penitence are de-emphasized and bliss and rejoicing are glorified by the Orthodox liturgy. The early Christian church was so joyful that it even permitted ritual dancing. A reminiscence of this practice survives in the Orthodox marriage rite, when the bride and groom are led three times around the altar by the priest in the "Dance of Isaiah."

The faith of the Eastern church is based not on the idea of God's justice, but of His love. Penance is not considered to be a way of compensating for sins, but simply a road to greater sanctity. Sin is not the breaking of laws, but a lessening of man's resemblance to God—a flaw in the "icon" of God. The priest is not considered spiritually superior to his parishioners. When conferring absolution he does not say, "I absolve you," as in the West, but only asks that God absolve them. It is through His love that God will bestow His grace equally on everyone, no matter how imperfect. The redemption made possible by Jesus Christ is for all men past and present, living and dead.

The Orthodox church has basically the same seven sacraments as the Roman Catholic church: Baptism, Chrismation (Confirmation), the Eucharist, Confession, Holy Orders, Marriage, and the Anointing of the Sick. Only bishops can confer Holy Orders. Priests can celebrate the other sacraments. There are also many "sacramentals," such as the service for the burial of the dead, plus a great many minor blessings for all occasions. Baptism is accomplished by a threefold immersion in water and is immediately followed by "Chrismation." The new church member is then allowed to take communion even if he or she is an infant. The Orthodox, like the Catholics, believe that during the Eucharist the bread and wine actually become the Body and Blood of Christ. Communion is generally taken about five times a year and confession is equally infrequent. Church members must fast before the Eucharist. During the four great fasting periods of the church year—Lent, Assumption, Christmas, and the Fast of the Apostles—the rules of fasting are more rigorous than those of any Western church. During Lent, for instance, not only is meat forbidden but so are fish and all animal products, as well as wine and oil. The anointing of the sick corresponds to Extreme Unction in the Catholic church, but it has two purposes—the forgiveness of sins and the restoration of bodily health—so it may be administered to the sick as well as the dying.

All members of the church—laymen, priests, bishops— are considered equal in importance, just as the Apostles were equal. Parish priests are often elected by their parishioners; bishops and patriarchs are generally elected by episcopal synods, but in some Orthodox churches the clergy and laity also participate in the election. An Orthodox priest may be married, but he must marry before taking his vows, and he may not remarry even if his wife dies. (Orthodox laymen are allowed no more than three marriages.) Those men who decide before their ordination to take a vow of celibacy become monks. Because canon law requires that bishops be celibate, all bishops are chosen from the ranks of the monks. Thus, no married priest can rise any higher in the church hierarchy. Because of this, it was long customary for Greek parish priests to receive only a rudimentary education, while higher education and theological training were reserved for the monks. This has had an unfortunate effect on the priests. In addition to their poor education, they have had to exist on pitifully small salaries, so that most village priests after ordination still must pursue another profession, such as farming or carpentry. Furthermore, the poor salaries have lowered the social position of the priests in the villages. Recently in the Greek church, however, there have been efforts to raise the educational level, salary, and social standing of the local priests. The life of a village priest is a demanding one. In addition to scraping together a living for himself and his family, he leads the divine liturgy every Sunday, visits the sick, and blesses every undertaking. In some villages he is the only person with any medical knowledge, so he must act as a doctor too. In spite of his many duties, the village priest manages to take a personal interest in the lives and tribulations of every one of his flock.

In Greece the Orthodox dioceses are kept small, as they were in the early church, and, as a result, the bishop often can have personal contact with the worshipers. The laity go to him not only for spiritual advice but for practical advice as well, and bishops often manage to arrange favors of a very practical nature for their parishioners. The bishop does a good deal of preaching and is often assisted in this task by a staff of monks or educated laymen, such as the local schoolteachers, who may well have studied theology in the university. The local priest does not usually preach sermons because he does not have the theological and educational background. It is not considered odd that laymen preach; all Greeks, whether they are members of the clergy or not, take a great interest in theology. Indeed, some of the greatest Greek theologians have been laymen.

There is a growing number of lay groups in Greece that devote themselves to evangelical and educational work. They publish magazines and books and have organized eight thousand catechism schools for children. One of these groups, *Zoe*, is made up of unmarried men who take no formal vows but must leave the brotherhood when they marry; about a quarter of the members are actually monks.

Orthodox churches are built in the form of a Greek cross, with a dome at the center and an icon of *Christ Pantocrator* ("all-ruling") inside the dome looking down. There are no pews or chairs; only some benches or stalls along the walls. The congregation stands and moves about during the long services, and worshipers come and go as they please, creating an atmosphere of informality and a sense of active participation quite different from that of Western churches. As in the primitive church, Orthodox services are chanted or sung. The Old Testament text used by the church is the ancient Greek translation, the Septuagint, which differs in some points from the original Hebrew. In addition to the books found in the Hebrew Old Testament, the Septuagint contains ten other books, the deuterocanonical books, which are generally considered to be less authoritative than the rest of the Old Testament. Instrumental music is not allowed because of the belief that man must praise God with his own voice, not with lifeless instruments. Early Greek Christians remembered how, in secret pagan rites, instruments such as the pipe and the drum drove the worshipers to orgiastic frenzies. Over the centuries, the Orthodox church has perfected choral singing of great difficulty and intricacy.

Like the early Christian church, the Orthodox church believes that the word of God should be taught in the native language of the people. Throughout Europe, the Near East, and Central Asia, many languages were first put in written form by Orthodox missionaries translating the Bible and the liturgy into the native language. In the ninth century two Greek monks from Thessalonica, Cyril and his brother Methodios, were chosen to convert the Slavs because they knew the Slavic dialect. They traveled throughout what is now Czechoslovakia and Bulgaria and accomplished the enormous task of translating the Bible into Slavonic, after first inventing a written alphabet for the language. The Cyrillic alphabet is the foundation of modern written Russian and other Slavonic languages.

The belief in preaching in the native language, although admirably democratic, has caused the church some difficulty. The various languages used in Orthodox churches led to the establishment of national churches, many of which ultimately developed differences from each other. The fact that each national church was self-governing and had its own head encouraged ties between the church and national government rather than a unity of Orthodox churches across national boundaries. This problem is well illustrated by the many emigrant Orthodox churches in the United States that have been plagued by nationalistic disputes and that persist in reciting services in the language of the father country—Armenian, Ukrainian, Russian, Greek, Arabic. As the immigrants' children grow up, however, a progressive breeze is blowing through the various Orthodox churches in the United States, and many of them have started presenting services in English as well as in the language of the father country.

The Greek "diaspora" is under the jurisdiction of the Patriarch of Constantinople. There are about 5 million Orthodox in North America. They are divided into about fifteen national groups, of which the Greek contingent numbers 2.8 million. Now that many other Orthodox churches in the United States have become bilingual, the Greek Orthodox have recognized the practice by making it permissible.

Athenagoras I, the Patriarch of Constantinople from 1949 to 1972, took dramatic steps to heal the schism with Rome. Two unprecedented meetings with Pope Paul VI were followed by the Patriarch's visit to Rome in 1967—a historic first—when the Pope expressed sorrow that "we cannot have that complete communion among ourselves which would be a sign to the world." The Patriarch, however, has no jurisdictional authority over the autocephalous branches of the Orthodox church, and it does not seem likely that either the laity or the clergy of the church of Greece will want reunion with Rome in the immediate future. Still, ecumenical talks continue between Rome and Constantinople and John Paul II made it a point, soon after he became Pope in 1978, to visit the Orthodox spiritual leader, Patriarch Demetrios I.

When Christianity supplanted the polytheistic religion of pagan Greece, the Greeks, with characteristic flexibility, incorporated elements of their old religion into the new one. Although the last pagan temples were closed in A.D. 392, the old gods were not completely forgotten. The shrine at Eleusis to the goddess Demeter became a shrine to a Christian saint, Dhimitra, who, as it happened, had been kidnaped and then restored to her mother just like Demeter, and who also had had a great influence on the fertility of the fields. Some characteristics of Dionysus, the pagan god of wine, reappeared in Saint Dionysius, who, when still a child, is said to have discovered a strange plant that turned out to be the grapevine.

Like the gods in ancient times, today's saints are often revered at shrines and tiny chapels. Many of these shrines are built in a spirit of thanksgiving for services rendered. Usually the size of a large birdhouse, there are thousands of them throughout Greece, often situated at the most picturesque bends in the road. Each shrine houses an icon with an oil lamp burning in front of it. Shrines to pagan gods were built in the same spots and for the same purpose—to provide the traveler with a moment of rest and prayerful meditation before resuming his journey. The roadside shrines are built by individuals who tend them and make sure there is enough oil to keep their lamps burning. Devout travelers will fuel the lamps, tend the wicks, and perhaps leave a contribution for the upkeep of the shrine in the small boxes provided for that purpose.

Westerners have often criticized the Orthodox faith for being mystical, ascetic, otherworldly, and not relevant in the life of today. Anyone who spends a good deal of time in Greece can testify that this is not so. The Greeks practice their religion as naturally and as continuously as they breathe, and they see nothing incongruous about calling on God to help them in everything from planting a crop to ridding a building of vermin. As G. Every said in *The Byzantine Patriarchate*, a religion so concerned with the practical aspects of man's life "can hardly be dismissed as pure mysticism."

SEVEN

Retsina
and
Moussaka

"If the pot boils, friendship lives."
GREEK PROVERB

Centuries before Christ, when the inhabitants of the rest of Europe were gnawing on half-cooked thigh bones of wild animals, the Greeks were feasting on such delicacies as roast lamb with capers, boiled sea-fowl eggs, rice flavored with saffron, lentil soup, honey cakes, Persian peaches, Oriental oranges, and various wines, some of them perfumed. The ancient Greeks had sophisticated sauces and made lavish use of herbs such as oregano, basil, bay leaves, dill, and mint, plus spices imported from the Orient.

Plato gravely discussed the writings of Philoxenus, who concerned himself with such questions as which kinds of fish should be baked and which boiled, and what size octopus is the most delectable. The earliest records of Greek dining habits reveal a characteristic that is just as true today. For a Greek, a meal is first of all a social occasion. Eating and drinking are a pleasant background for conversation, gossip, debate, and to eat alone is unthinkable.

In classical Greece, when guests were present, women were banished from the table. Servants washed the hands and feet of guests and even perfumed their hair. The diners lounged on couches and ate with their hands. The meal might be a symposium; each man would speak in turn about some intellectual matter while the others listened, and a "symposiarch" moderated. Or the guests might be diverted by the performances of acrobats, dancing girls, and musicians.

Not surprisingly, Greek cuisine early spread to neighboring countries. Roman conquerors brought Greek cooks back to Italy. Lucullus, the Roman general of the first century B.C. famed for his lavish banquets, founded his reputation on Greek cuisine. There is evidence that the famous *bouillabaisse* of France was introduced to Marseilles by seafaring Greeks, who called it *kakavia*. In the second century A.D., Athenaeus, a native of Egypt who lived in Rome, recorded all the various methods of cooking in a book called the *Deipnosophists* (*Banquet of the Learned*). He described many aspects of Greek cuisine that are still common today. For example, herbs were used on meat and fish, oil and vinegar dressing was popular, and the delicious tiny meatballs called *keftedes* were standard fare. During the Middle Ages, the art of Greek cooking was refined to perfection in the Orthodox monasteries. While preparing meals, the cooking monks wore a white version of the tall, brimless, black monk's cap—in other words, what is still today the traditional headgear of master chefs. Although the Greek people themselves have been changed over the centuries by wars and conquerors, Greek cooking has altered surprisingly little. It has evolved, but many of the dishes served now would have been familiar to Socrates and Pericles. By comparison, French *haute cuisine* could be considered an upstart.

Geographically Greece belongs as much to the West as to the East, but its cuisine is almost entirely Eastern. With the rest of the Middle East, Greece shares a culinary tradition built on lamb as the staple meat and olive oil as the basic fat. Other cornerstones of Middle Eastern cooking are rice, figs, yogurt, coarse whole-meal bread at every meal, shish kebab, and complicated dishes of ground meat mixed with spices, rice, and herbs and often stuffed into vegetables or wrapped in leaves. Middle Eastern traders became rich on the spice trade between the Orient and Europe, and in the process incorporated many of the exotic seasonings into their own food. Popular throughout Greece and the Middle East are the very sweet pastries that are magnificent examples of the pastry cook's art. They are made from many layers of paper-thin dough called *filo*, filled with chopped nuts, and drenched in honey. These pastries are never eaten as desserts, but are served as treats for guests on special occasions or as afternoon or late-night snacks.

Many travel books on Greece lament the fact that the true excellence of Greek cooking can be sampled only in private homes and not in the country's restaurants, which tend to offer either simple working-class dishes or mediocre attempts at continental cooking for tourists. This may have been true once, but things have changed. In Athens and its environs there are now restaurants specializing in the best native Greek dishes. The Taverna Ta Nissia in the lower level of the Athens Hilton has an admirable and well-researched menu of the traditional dishes of the Greek islands. Several good Greek restaurants in Athens offer a taverna-like ambiance but much better food than is generally found in tavernas. Diners are given no choice but are served a long series of *mezedakia* (singular *mezes*)—small plates of delicacies. A meal might begin with salty *taramosalata*—a pâté made of cod's roe—or perhaps with little pies of cheese, spinach, or seafood wrapped in flaky pastry. There will be the traditional Greek salad of lettuce, radishes, cu-

cumbers, tomatoes, scallions, black olives, chunks of white
feta cheese, and anchovies, all mixed together with a vinaigrette sauce and sprinkled with fresh mint. Next might
come crisply fried tiny squid and fried eggplant, seasonal
seafood dishes, and rice-stuffed grape leaves with an egg
and lemon sauce, tiny sausages wrapped in pastry, and
shrimp in ingenious variations. Finally there might be roast
lamb or stuffed capon, if anyone is still hungry. Eating in
these restaurants provides the best broad introduction to
Greek cuisine.

Two such restaurants in Athens are Mirtia, on the hill
above the Stadium, and Steki Tou Yianni, in the quarter of
Athens called Kipseli. In both, strolling musicians play and
sing popular Greek songs with frequent assistance from the
diners. (Both tend to close for long periods in July and
August, like many other Athenian restaurants, so it is wise
to check before going.) Vassilenas, in Piraeus, offers a
sixteen-course meal that is almost certain to defeat the most
devoted gourmand, even though he may have fasted all day.
The best place to find Anatolian-style Greek cooking is
Gerofinikas (Old Pine Tree) on Pindarou Street, at the end
of a nondescript-looking alley lined with cubicles that once
housed a brothel. Inside are gleaming copper braziers, linen-
draped tables, and an irresistible assortment of Oriental
Greek specialties displayed like works of art in the spotless
glass showcases, such as the unsurpassed rice orientale and
ekmek kataif. It is a favorite restaurant of many knowledge-
able Athenians, and reservations are essential.

In a simple working-class restaurant, a meal might con-
sist of a plate of boiled mountain herbs, a plate of the huge
kidney-shaped beans, *gigantes*, in a vinaigrette sauce, a
Greek salad, a dish of chicken in tomato sauce with rice
pilaf, and a dish of fried squid—all shared by several people. When a Greek goes to his neighborhood taverna for a

glass of the strong, anise-flavored *ouzo*, he will be served a plate filled, perhaps, with chunks of feta cheese, cucumbers, tomatoes, and the shiny black olives. This again is *mezedakia*. The word is usually translated as "appetizers," but it means something small, delectable, and part of a large selection.

A Greek would never dream of drinking without eating something at the same time. This may be one reason why Greeks are rarely seen drunk. The exception to this rule is the famous wine festival at Daphni, held every autumn. For a small entrance fee one may stroll around the grounds, glass in hand, sampling hundreds of Greek wines from huge casks and participating in the general pandemonium. The festival evokes the image of a pagan bacchanal. Modern drama has its roots in similar festivals held centuries ago to honor Dionysus, the god of wine. He was believed to live in a vineyard along with satyrs who were half-goat and half-man. During the early festivals, revelers dressed in goatskins would sing. These men were called *tragos-oidos* or "goat-singers." The word ultimately gave us "tragedy," and the celebrating pagans evolved into the chorus and principals of Greek drama.

The national drink of Greece is *ouzo*, a strong Pernod-like clear spirit that is distilled from the residue of the grapes left after the wine is made. When ice or water is added, the *ouzo* turns milky white. The *retsina*, or resinated white wines, are the *vins du pays* (*retsina* rosé is called *kokkineli*). Since ancient times, the Greeks have drunk wines pungent with the sharp tang of resin. Some say this is because the original wine casks were made of pine, which leaked resin into the wine, and that the Greeks got used to the taste. Others say that the ancients added resin to prolong the life of the wine. Although the Greeks have acquired a taste for *retsina* over the centuries, many visitors will not find it to their liking. There are many excellent and inexpensive non-resinated Greek wines, however, that provide a perfect complement to the robust Greek food. These include Santa Helena, a dry white wine; Demestica, a light white wine; Naoussa, a full-bodied red; Roditys, a surprisingly dry rosé; and Mavrodaphni, a sweet, dark purple wine. Monte Nero is an outstanding smooth red wine rarely found outside the country.

Before taking the first sip, a Greek never fails to clink his glass against those of his companions and to make a toast, usually "*Yiassas*"—"Your health." The clinking of glasses stems from an ancient Greek belief that wine should be savored with all the five senses. It delights the nose with its bouquet, the eye with its color, the touch and taste with its body and flavor and, because of the clinking of glasses, even the ear.

Every day in Greece is arranged to allow for the maximum amount of enjoyment and good fellowship. After a morning of work, everything shuts down during a leisurely lunch that takes place at 2:00 or 2:30 or even later. Then everyone takes a siesta until 5:00 or 5:30 before returning to work for a few more hours. There is time for a visit to a coffee house or a *taverna* before dinner, which is served around 10:00 P.M. or later. Another visit to a coffee house, *taverna*, or perhaps, in the summer, an outdoor movie concludes the day. The afternoon siesta gives Greeks the strength to stay up until the early morning hours, yet be at work by 8:30 A.M. after a cup of strong Turkish coffee.

When Greeks go out to eat, they can choose from a number of different kinds of establishments, each with its own specialty. There is the *zacharoplasteion*, or sweet shop, some of which are vast. On warm summer nights in Athens it looks as though the entire population is sitting outdoors enjoying the air and the company while eating honey-sweet

flaky *baklava* and sipping tiny cups of thick Turkish coffee.
Then there is the *psistarya* or rotisserie, which has a mini-
mum of amenities but does one thing very well—charcoal-
roasted lamb. The skewered lambs rotate on their spits in
front of the gaudy, neon-lighted restaurants. Along with the
crusty, aromatic lamb that is carved from the spit and
served at bare wooden tables, customers are given a simple
Greek salad, the ubiquitous bread, and the husky red house
wine. Tavernas range from the most humble—a couple of
tables and some casks of wine in a small village square—to
the very elaborate ones that maintain a rustic taverna-type
decor in the midst of Athens. The Plaka section of the city
is crowded with noisy tavernas that spill out onto the roofs
in the summer. All tavernas offer food and drink; some
provide *bouzouki* music and entertainment as well. Many
of the noisiest tavernas in the Plaka are no more than tourist
traps, but those Athenians who want to skip the belly dancers and glossy decor and concentrate on good food and
authentic old Plaka atmosphere go to the venerable taverna
Xynou, and choose from among the pots in the kitchen.
Xynou offers excellent food, intimate rooms, wall murals
of old Athens, strolling musicians, and a pleasant outdoor
garden all for a modest price.

Perhaps the most charming tavernas are those by the
seaside. The 2,500-mile coastline of Greece is dotted with
tavernas serving fresh from the sea such delicacies as small
red mullet (*barbouni*) and sea bass (*plaki*) braised with vegetables. The exquisite curving yacht harbor of Tourkolimano in Piraeus is lined with waterside tavernas. (Many
patriotic Greeks now call it Mikrolimano, small harbor,
instead of "Turkish harbor.") Diners walk across the road
to the kitchen of the restaurant, where they select the fish
or seafood—usually still alive—that they want. Customers
are charged by the weight of their choice. While their selec-

tion is being cooked, the diners return to their tables at the waterside, where strolling hawkers sell them cooked shellfish to begin the meal, and a crowd of fat cats begs for leftovers.

In almost every Greek restaurant and taverna it is not only permitted, but customary, for guests to choose their dinners by going into the kitchen and looking into the pots.

The ceremonies of life in Greece and the events of the church year are all intimately linked to special foods. At Christmas, the family and guests are treated to *kourabiedes* (sweet, buttery shortbread cookies) and *Christopsomo* (Christmas bread—decorated with walnuts, sesame seeds, and a cross made of dough). Other sweet breads, like the deep-fried *loukoumades*, are popular during the Christmas season. January 1, Saint Basil's Day, is as important as Christmas to the Greeks. They exchange gifts on this day, and practice a number of rituals designed to gauge the fortunes of the coming year. The customs include cutting open a pomegranate and counting the seeds to see how much abundance is in store. At midnight on New Year's Eve, every Greek family eats a *Vasilopeta*—Saint Basil's cake— in which a coin, often gold, was embedded before baking. The head of the house cuts the cake, setting aside the first piece for Christ and the next for Saint Basil. The third is for the head of the house, and so on in order of age. Whoever gets the coin will, of course, have good luck for the coming year. If the coin is found in the piece for Christ or Saint Basil, it goes to the church. Another charming Greek custom is to grow a pot of sweet basil on the balcony, terrace, or courtyard of every house. It serves several purposes: it is sacred to Saint Basil, it keeps flies and mosquitoes away, and it is useful in cooking.

The Easter season is the religious and culinary apex of the Greek year. The last week before the beginning of Lent is called *Apokrea*—the Greek carnival. Greeks fast during the first and last weeks of Lent, and the most devout fast for the entire forty days, often abstaining from fish, eggs, butter, milk, and cheese as well as meat, and on some days avoiding wine and olive oil too. They get by on ascetic meals of boiled beans, raw onions, olives, bread, and *halvah* —the Turkish sweet made of sugar, oil, almonds, and semolina or farina. On Holy Thursday, lambs are killed and hung, and eggs are boiled, dyed red to signify the blood of Christ, and polished with olive oil until they shine. Lentil soup is the traditional Holy Thursday supper. On Holy Friday, the *Lambropsomo* (sometimes called *Tsoureki*) or Easter bread is baked. It is a sweet, braided bread topped with some of the red eggs. On Saturday, the men supervise the preparations for roasting the family's lamb on huge spits in the village roasting pit and lighten their labor with a good supply of *retsina*. Meanwhile, the women use the entrails of the lamb to make the traditional Easter soup, *mayeritsa*, and the Easter sausage, *kokoretsi*. On the night of Holy Saturday, everyone goes to church carrying unlighted candles. The church is in darkness and the suspense mounts. Exactly at midnight, the priest appears from behind the altar screen holding a lighted candle and announces "*Christos anesti*"—"Christ is risen." The moment is one of high emotion, and is often marked with fireworks and cheers. Everyone lights his candle from his neighbor's and wends his way homeward, sheltering his candle flame from the wind. At home, the strict fast of the last week of Lent ends with a midnight supper of Easter bread, eggs, and cheese and the delicately flavored *mayeritsa*. To make this soup, the entrails of the lamb are cooked in a stock seasoned with scallions and fresh dill. The tart egg and lemon sauce, *avgolemono*, is beaten in at the last moment. The next day, Easter Sunday, the paschal lamb has the place of honor at the feast. It has been heavily seasoned with bits of garlic inserted into the meat and sprinkled with plenty of oregano.

The rituals of hospitality are as devoutly followed as the rituals of the church, and food always plays a part in them. Whatever the occasion—a baptism, wedding, death, name day, feast, or just unexpected visitors—the woman of the house must rise to the occasion with the appropriate food, for her reputation is at stake. After a funeral, the surviving members of the family traditionally eat a meal of fish and drink wine and Turkish coffee. Memorial services are held on the fortieth day, and on the first and third anniversaries of the death. For these occasions a sweet called *kolyva* is made from boiled wheat (signifying everlasting life), raisins (signifying sweetness), and pomegranate seeds (signifying plenty). Before it is eaten it is blessed in the church.

Making and serving Turkish coffee is also surrounded with a great deal of ritual. Shopkeepers of all kinds frequently offer their customers coffee as a gesture of hospitality, and coffee shops and sweet shops are the favorite spot for relaxation, refreshment, and conversation at any time of the day. According to purists, Turkish coffee can be brewed with thirty-six different degrees of sweetness. When he orders his coffee, a Greek always specifies whether he wants it *glikos* (very sweet), *metrios* (medium), *schetos* (black), or some variation of the three. The coffee is brewed one cup at a time in a small, long-handled, hourglass-shaped brass or copper pot, a *briki*. The mixture of water, sugar, and powdered coffee is boiled until it almost foams out of the pot. The amount of foam or *kaimak* it forms is very important—the more foam, the better the coffee. The cup is only half-drained, until the muddy grounds are reached. Greeks, especially the women, sometimes turn the cup over into the saucer and then tell fortunes from the patterns made by the grounds.

Every Greek family will lavish food on a guest, even if it means slaughtering the family's only chicken or going without meat for a month to do it. Guests who might be watching their weight or eating lightly for any other reason will receive no sympathy from a Greek hostess. There is an Arab saying that is no less true in Greece: "The food equals the affection." What it means is: "If you don't eat at least three helpings of my food, preferably more, you don't love me." The only way to avoid being put to such a test is to pay calls in the middle of the afternoon (in Greece that's 6:00 P.M.) or well after dinner, when only coffee, drinks, sweets, or a few *mezedakia* will be brought out.

Although such complicated dishes as *moussaka*—the eggplant and minced-meat casserole topped with a bécha-mel sauce—or poultry stuffed with mixtures of meat, spices, fruits, nuts, and rice are among the glories of Greek cuisine, many visitors remember most fondly the plain coarse foods of the small villages. Often those meals were eaten in breathtaking outdoor surroundings that add more than any sauce to the food. As with the Easter lamb, Greeks let nothing go to waste. They can make a feast out of wild mountain herbs like chicory or dandelions, wild figs or sea urchins—all of which they can gather on walks. They pluck bay leaves off the trees for seasoning, and make a delicious stew, *stefado*, from wild rabbit. Bean soup is called the meat of the villager, and the traditional Friday night meal in the villages is bean soup with a tomato base, accompanied by coarse bread, raw onions, and vegetables pickled in brine. The secret weapons of every Greek cook are oregano, cin-namon, garlic, and spearmint, all used sparingly in unex-pected but delicious ways.

Village women manage to produce miraculous baked and roasted dishes by using primitive beehive-shaped ovens that are built outside the house and stoked with coals from a brushwood fire. Women who don't have ovens take their food to be cooked to the *fourno*—the village bakery. Even in the middle of Athens, housewives whose oven will not accommodate a large cut of meat or a large batch of Easter bread will use the neighborhood *fourno*. It is a common sight to see a boy carrying a steaming leg of lamb or tray of hot breads home to his mother.

The fruit in Greece is a delight to visitors. In winter and spring, there are marvelously juicy oranges, originally brought to the country from the Orient, followed by apples and pears. In summer, there are cherries as large as plums, strawberries, apricots, and yellow peaches. In autumn, there is the *peponi*—a Greek melon halfway between a cantaloupe and a honeydew—and watermelon (*karpouzi*). White, russet, and amber grapes hang in heavy clusters from the arbors, waiting to be picked, or turning into raisins on the vine, while the figs (*sika*), bursting with sweet purple juice, are equally plentiful. Hawkers of fruit fill the early autumn mornings with their cries and housewives boil the ripe fruits in sugar syrup, turning them into spoon sweets for the guests that the winter holidays will bring.

EIGHT

Syrtaki
and
Bouzouki

When a Greek is sitting in his favorite taverna, enjoying good food, good wine, and the companionship of his friends, he is filled with a sense of well-being and high spirits that the Greeks call *kefi*. When the *kefi* reaches a certain pitch, he can no longer contain the urge to express his satisfaction with life in general, so he gets up and begins to dance. Dancing has been an essential part of every Greek's life since before the beginning of recorded history. Archaeological evidence shows that as early as the fifteenth century B.C. religious ceremonies involved dances that must have borne a marked resemblance to the dances executed today in the tavernas and village squares.

Originally, the dance was a part of the worship of primitive gods. Later, dances were also used to incite men to fight and to condition soldiers and sailors to work in perfect unison, following unspoken commands transmitted by touch. In Greece, all the ceremonies of life have their own dances, some gay, some solemn. Even today, in many villages dancing on holidays and festivals provides young girls with their only opportunity to display their grace and beauty while the young men show off their physical strength and agility. (Women are traditionally expected to dance with great dignity—never doing the fast steps.) Every region of Greece has its own dances, although in recent years they have been disseminated throughout the country by traveling troupes of professional dancers. The pagan origin of some of the dances is still evident. Twenty years ago, in the fields of Epirus, it was possible to see girls re-enacting the death and rebirth of nature with ancient songs and dances. The sword dance that is still performed in Crete was described by Homer in the *Iliad*. In classical Greece, mastering Terpsichore's art was considered a most important attribute for children of the higher classes, and many well-born young Athenians were renowned for their dancing prowess.

The dances of Greece are generally divided into two groups: the *syrto* dances, which are slow and dignified, with their dragging and shuffling steps, and the *pedecto* dances, which include hopping, jumping, stamping, leaping, or springing steps. Most often Greek dances are performed by a number of participants forming an open circle or a line, and moving counterclockwise. The leader demonstrates his skill by improvising, while the rest of the line does the basic step, almost like a chorus. There are hundreds of Greek dances, often with regional names and slight variations. Among the many professional companies that can be seen demonstrating these dances, the most notable is the troupe of Dora Stratou, which performs at an open-air theater on a hillside near the Acropolis. Some purists, however, feel that the professional dancers have lost the ability to improvise. A visit to almost any taverna in the Plaka, the old section of Athens, is certain to provide the visitor with the spectacle of ordinary Greeks doing the dances according to their own feelings.

The five best-known Greek dances are the *Kalamatiano*, the *Tsamiko*, the *Zeibekiko*, the *Hasapiko*, and the *Syrtaki*. The gay and carefree *Kalamatiano* is often considered the national dance of Greece. Its name recalls its place of origin near the town of Kalamata in the Peloponnesus. The dance is performed by a number of people moving in a line, with each dancer holding his neighbor's hand. The elbows are bent at right angles and the hands are held at shoulder height so that the arms form a W pattern. The leader performs intricate variations of the basic slow-quick-quick side step.

The *Tsamiko* is also a line dance performed by a group. Originating in Epirus, it is sometimes called the handkerchief dance because the leader and the second dancer firmly grasp opposite ends of a handkerchief. The dance is slow, dignified, and warlike, but at its peak the leader is expected to perform outstanding acrobatic feats, for which he gets support from the handkerchief held by the second dancer. It was a favorite dance of the mountain fighters during the War of Independence. Although this is a dance primarily for men, women do participate in the nonacrobatic steps.

The *Zeibekiko*, *Hasapiko*, and *Syrtaki* are also chiefly danced by men, although nowadays women are allowed to join in. The *Zeibekiko*, a favorite dance in the tavernas, is either a solo or is performed by two persons dancing face to face. This is the dance Anthony Quinn performed in the film *Zorba the Greek*. The dancer's arms are outstretched, resembling the wings of a bird, which is why it is frequently called the dance of the eagle. The *Zeibekiko* is a slow-moving dance of combat in which two men circle each other or, if there is only one performer, he dances around an imaginary antagonist. It is the most difficult of all Greek folk dances, because it depends entirely on the dancer's interpretation. He moves as if in a trance, his eyes cast down and his manner introspective. No matter how great his virtuosity, any applause or acknowledgment from onlookers would be considered a breach of etiquette, because he is dancing for himself alone. Often the dancer will hiss, a sound that some say derives from the hissing of large birds on the attack, or even, perhaps, the hissing of a snake.

The other popular taverna dance is the *Hasapiko* (butcher's dance). It apparently originated in the waterfront tavernas, where the *bouzouki* music would inspire two or three men to get up and dance, their arms on each other's shoulders. The number of dancers is limited to no more than three because the leader must instantly telegraph his variations on the basic movements by the touch of his hand on the shoulders of his neighbor. The movements are slow and moody. The dancers, their eyes downcast, are lost in their art, the celebration of the wine and the company. The version of the *Hasapiko* generally seen in Greece today is a simplified form of the dance, called the *Syrtaki*, which may be performed by as many as five. Although the same basic steps are used in both dances, the style and mood vary considerably. While the *Hasapiko* is tense and concentrated, performed to release pent up emotions, the *Syrtaki* is loose and bouncy and aimed for audience approval.

While women join in dancing both the *Hasapiko* and the *Syrtaki*, the basic steps are firm, precise, and decidedly masculine. But there is a feminine equivalent called the *Tsiphte Teli*, a lively and sensuous belly dance that came to Greece from Asia Minor. The decidedly effeminate movements do not dissuade men from joining in, imitating the women's actions with swaying hips, undulating arms, and trembling shoulders.

Dancing for Greeks is not merely an enjoyable form of self-expression; as sociologist Ted Petrides writes, it is a way of holding on to sanity in a world full of suffering and deprivation. Nikos Kazantzakis tells how his hero Zorba, in great grief at his son's death, got up and started dancing: "The others said 'Zorba's gone mad.' But I knew if I didn't dance at that moment I would go mad."

The accompaniment to the taverna dances is led by the *bouzouki*—the mandolin-like instrument that has been made famous by the music for such films as *Never on Sunday*. Equally important is the clarinet, on which the musicians produce uniquely Greek tonal variations. The violin is also popular for dances, and in Crete a special variation of it, the *lyra* (lyre or Cretan violin), is played with a bow. The *bouzouki* and the violin are descended from the ancient lyre (Apollo's instrument) while the clarinet evolved from the reed pipe used during the worship of Dionysus. The most ecstatic rites of Dionysus introduced such percussion instruments as drums, tambourines, hand and foot clappers, and cymbals. Other ancient instruments still played in Greece today are the *gaida,* a bagpipe of goatskin; the *pipiza* or *zournas,* a reed instrument with a piercing sound; the *floghera* (flute) the *santouri,* a type of dulcimer played with a small, padded hammer; and the *outi,* a large-bellied stringed instrument resembling a lute.

Like all other aspects of cultural life, Greek music stagnated during the Turkish occupation. Only the folk songs continued to develop. Many Greeks left their villages and homes to join roving bands that lived in the mountains. These warriors were called *klephts* (bandits) by the Turks. Each band of *klephts* had its own minstrels who composed and improvised songs that told of the band's battles, defeats, and heroic deeds. Other folk songs emerged throughout Greece during the Turkish period, each reflecting the character of the area where it originated. The songs of the islands, for example, had a charm and a smoothness of tone and rhythm not found in the *klephtic* ballads. On the plains and in valleys the songs were slow and relaxed, in the mountains proud and vigorous. They chronicled the lives of an enslaved people—the need for love, the struggle for freedom, the enjoyment of simple pleasures, the suffering that man endures. There were folk songs for every occasion—lullabies, nuptial songs, feasting songs, songs of the seasons. Mourning songs, called *myroloyia*, were sung by professional mourners who accented every line with wails and shrieks that would shake the hardest heart. They are among the most expressive and most moving of the songs written during the Turkish occupation, as can be seen in the following dirge from the Maini area in the Peloponnesus:

> My little cypress tree, so tall,
> About whose roots cold water stands
> From whose crown
> A golden cross now shows
> My little rock, my boulder,
> My little closet, locked,
> To you I told my secret
> Whenever I had need.
>
> But listen to me, wizened face,
> And, ah, my wisest head,
> My vault, as like the heavens,
> For all of us, our race—
> Go now, my good one, go
> To Saint Elias church
> And bring them with you
> And come back
> Where yet we wait for you.

Besides these folk songs, the only music Greeks heard during the Turkish period were the monophonic Byzantine chants sung in church. Because most Greeks were diligent churchgoers and knew most of the hymns by heart, church music exerted considerable influence on the style of the folk songs.

When Greece became an independent state in 1829, European influences engulfed Greece, or at least urban Greece. Greek musicians in the emerging cities turned their backs on their Byzantine and folk traditions and adopted the musical style of Italy, their nearest European neighbor. From the middle of the nineteenth century to the end of World War I, the words of the songs heard in Athens were Greek, but the music, in the cantata form, was so Italian that it might have been written in Venice or Naples. After World War I, Greece and most of the rest of Europe were gripped by a new rhythm from Spain—the tango. Urban Greeks adopted the tango as wholeheartedly as they had the cantata, and they held on to it for thirty years, even though it was totally alien to the Greek character. Modern Greek composers feel that this century of preoccupation with foreign rhythms greatly harmed musical development in Greece. "The romantic shallowness and melodic vulgarity of the cantata corrupted musically many generations of young Greeks," Mikis Theodorakis, the composer of the music for Z and Zorba the Greek, wrote a few years ago. "While the tango might have been a positive force in Spain, transported to other countries it became cheap, counterfeit, and commercial." Fortunately neither the tango nor the cantata took hold among the peasants in the countryside and, as more and more of them moved to the cities, they brought with them a new sound that is as Greek as feta cheese.

The *bouzouki* songs that most people associate with

Greek music today are part of this sound. These songs, called *rebetika* in Greek, have their roots in Byzantine hymns, old folk songs, and Oriental rhythms nurtured for centuries by Anatolian Greeks. The *rebetika* emerged from the lowest levels of urban life—the opium dens, the waterfront dives, the slums—where the European rhythms never took over. Instead, these urban outposts developed a new form out of the old musical traditions they knew. Originally, the *rebetika* dwelt on sordid themes common to the environment that produced them. "I am a rascal and a bum," one early song began, "and I enter the opium den still high from the night before." Greeks are rather puritanical about such subjects, and it seems surprising that they should respond to these songs. But they could not help it. The natural beauty of the music, with its traditional Greek sounds, filtered out of the opium dens and waterfront dives to the tavernas, the city squares, and the towns and villages beyond. The original sordid themes were abandoned for subjects that reflected the dreams, hopes, and apprehensions of the majority of Greeks. The main characteristic of the *rebetika* is the close harmony of music and poetry. The songs contain the best elements of all the musical movements that have touched Greece over the past five hundred years and blend them into a beautiful new sound. To the dominant influences of folk songs and Byzantine hymns are added restrained doses of harmony characteristic of the cantata but missing from traditional Greek music. The *rebetika* have also been influenced by the main instrument on which they are played, the *bouzouki*, whose melodic embellishments give the songs their special sound.

Love is a dominant theme of the *rebetika*, as it is in all vocal music. In these songs the lover always speaks simply and poetically:

In the paths of life,
By your stately staircase
I fly around like a bat
Seeking consolation and hope.

But love is not the only subject of the *rebetika*, as it is of most popular songs of other countries. There is a song about a watch, for example, and another about worry beads. The misery of the poor is captured beautifully in a song that begins, "Every step of my life is full of pain and anguish." Another song speaks of loneliness:

The moon is down
The darkness is deep
Only one man
Cannot fall asleep.

The *rebetika* have had the most profound influence on Greek music in this century. "With the single exception of jazz," writes music historian Markos Dragounis, "the modern world from Greece westward has not produced anything which so convincingly and authentically expresses the soul of simple people and their yearnings." The similarities of *rebetika* to jazz and the blues are many. Both jazz and *rebetika* grew in the underbellies of cities—brothels, drug dens, and bars. Both the blues and *rebetika* bemoan the grim realities of life—poverty, drink, narcotics, disease, disloyalty, and early death—with a kind of grim stoicism. Only since World War II have the *rebetika* emerged from the hash dens, seamen's bars, and brothels of Greek port cities, where the songs were sung and enjoyed by a picturesque underworld element scorned by all respectable Greeks.

The growing popularity of *rebetika* has spread with the

Greek diaspora of Greek laborers to foreign countries. In Greek clubs and tavernas in New York, Sydney, Stuttgart, and Cape Town, Greeks who spend the week as factory workers, housepainters, and short-order cooks find solace from too much work, too little money, and the aching homesickness that Greeks call *xenitia*, which is also the title of a famous rebetic song:

> The foreign life is making me old
>   and eating me alive.
> I can't stand it, Mana, my
>   body's wearing out.
> The foreign life holds sorrow
>   and so much bitterness.
> It feeds on young men's lives
>   and wastes poor bodies.

Greece's best modern composers—Manos Hadjidakis, Mikis Theodorakis, Stavros Xerhakis, and George Hadjinassios—have been greatly influenced by *rebetika*, folk songs, Byzantine music, and other traditional themes. In addition to composing music, Theodorakis, an avowed Marxist and a Greek Communist Party deputy in Parliament, is a political activist whose beliefs are often reflected in his songs. The other three are not directly involved in politics, although Hadjidakis frequently voices his disdain for the excesses of Greek leftists. Hadjidakis is popular in Greece for both his songs and his serious music. He won an Oscar for the theme music in *Never on Sunday*, which starred actress Melina Mercouri, another political activist who became minister of culture under Premier Andreas Papandreou.

The feeling the best *rebetika* impart was well expressed by Hadjidakis when he described the moment he first heard one of them: "Dazed by the grandeur and depth of the melodic phrases, a stranger to them, young and without strength, I believed suddenly that the song I was listening to was my own, utterly my own story."

NINE

Athens—
"A Divine Work!"

> "For Athens alone of her contemporaries is
> found when tested to be greater than her
> reputation."
> PERICLES

Athens is the oldest and the newest capital in Europe. The Acropolis and the ruins around it testify to its place as the first city of the ancient world. But except for these monuments, Athens seems younger than most cities in the New World—as indeed it is. Athens became the capital of modern Greece in 1834, thirty-five years after Washington, D.C., became the capital of the United States. In 1834, when the seat of government was moved from Nauplia to Athens, the city numbered only three hundred houses and a few churches. Everything else has been built since then, most of it in the last fifty years.

Throughout its roller-coaster history, Athens has always fascinated visitors. In antiquity, its reputation was so great and so envied by other cities that when Pindar, a citizen of Thebes, wrote an ode calling it the "Shining, violet-crowned, song-famed bulwark of Greece," his jealous fellow Thebans fined him 10,000 drachmas. Even when Athens was reduced to a small village during its long captivity by the Turks, Europeans were still fascinated by it, as is

143

shown by the following lines from Shelley's *Ode to Liberty* written twenty-three centuries after Pindar:

A divine work! Athens, diviner yet,
  Gleamed with its crest of columns, on the will
Of man, as on a mount of diamond, set.

The growth of the city to its present size of 3 million people was accelerated in 1923 when many of the 1.5 million Greek refugees from Asia Minor settled in Athens, and again after the civil war of the late 1940s, when thousands of villagers began moving to the capital. Athens, then, is essentially a new city, a bustling boom town built around monuments of a brilliant past. While the monuments initially attract most visitors to Athens, it is the city itself and its vitality that move many to return again and again. Modern Athens is not as imposing as Rome, as enchanting as Paris, as stately as London, or as lively as New York. But it is more human than any of them. In no other place I know can one enjoy all the pleasures of urban living and yet feel so close to people and nature. Every neighborhood in the city is like a little village. People pour into the neighborhood squares to sit for hours and eat, drink, talk, laugh, and debate. Through every open window in Athens comes the scent of basil from a hundred balconies, pine and myrtle from a dozen hills, and sea air from the nearby Aegean. A person can leave the center of Athens and in twenty minutes find himself swimming in the sea or looking down from the peak of a mountain.

Athens lies on a plain between the Aegean and three low mountains that are spread in an arc. Mt. Parnes, the highest of the three, lies to the north; Mt. Pentelicon, which supplied most of the marble for the Acropolis, is in the east; and Mt. Hymettus, bare above slopes of fragrant bushes

and flowers, curves toward the sea in the south. The city
fans out from Syntagma (Constitution) Square, a broad
plaza rimmed by travel agencies, luxury hotels, and outdoor
cafés. The square is dominated by the former royal palace
that stands on an incline at its eastern end. The palace,
which was converted into the Parliament building in 1933,
is neither distinguished nor garish and serves as a properly
somber backdrop for the Tomb of the Unknown Soldier
directly below it. The tomb is decorated by a relief of a
helmeted naked warrior and is guarded by soldiers who
periodically emerge from their sentry boxes to execute fault-
less marching maneuvers. To the south of the tomb, Amalia
Avenue leads past the beautiful National Gardens and Zap-
pion Park to Syngrou Avenue, which continues to the coast,
the airport, and the beaches. On the other side of the tomb,
Queen Sofia Avenue leads eastward past government buildings, embassies, and the Athens Hilton toward the verdant
suburbs of Kephisia and Ekali. Behind the Parliament building and the gardens are rows of luxury apartment buildings
and the presidential palace guarded by *evzones*, the royal
guard dressed in red caps and full white pleated skirts called
fustanellas.

The northern side of Syntagma Square is connected by
two parallel avenues to Omonia (Concord) Square—a wide
circle with a fountain in the center and surrounded by hotels
and office buildings. Half a dozen streets lead away from
Omonia like the spokes of a wheel—one toward Piraeus,
another toward Corinth, a third to the National Archaeological Museum. Syntagma is essentially European; Omonia
is purely Greek. Syntagma belongs to the tourists, the dip-
lomats, the wealthy and educated Greeks. Omonia belongs
to the workers, the clerks, the transplanted villagers. Syntagma contains the offices of most of the airlines, while
Omonia is the center of the underground railway to the

suburbs and working districts. Restaurants in Syntagma feature lobster thermidor and chicken Talleyrand. The tavernas in Omonia offer *kokoretsi* (liver wrapped in lamb intestines) and kebab on a spit. The two streets that connect the square are Stadiou, sometimes known as Churchill, and Panepistimiou, also known as Venizelou. Stadiou, the narrower, is lined with office buildings and stores. Panepistimiou is a wide, airy street lined with expensive restaurants, jewelry stores, banks, theaters, and the neoclassical buildings of the University of Athens.

Above Panepistimiou is Kolonaki, the aristocratic quarter of Athens, built around its own small but elegant square at the base of Mt. Lycabettus, a sharp peak jutting unexpectedly above the city where Athena is said to have dropped it by accident. An underground cable car makes the ascent to the top in less than three minutes. Passengers emerge to find a charming white church, a bell tower, and an outdoor café surrounded by landscaped terraces. There is a spectacular view of Athens and its environs all the way to the sea. The view is clearest, and the famous Greek light at its most beautiful, early in the morning or late in the afternoon. On Easter eve, the church is packed to overflowing with worshipers attending the midnight service. After it, the crowd files down the slope, each person bearing a twinkling candle and trying to keep the flame alive until he reaches home. The serpentine line of tiny lights makes Lycabettus from a distance look like a colossal Christmas tree in the middle of the city.

The main Easter service is held at the Athens Cathedral in a small square two blocks west of Syntagma. The cathedral was built between 1840 and 1855 with material from seventy-two churches destroyed by the Moslems, and it is not particularly impressive. But the small church of Aghios Eleftherios right next to it is a fine example of eleventh-century architecture. On Metropolis Street, which connects the cathedral to Syntagma, is a tiny chapel sheltered by the overhanging façade of a new office building: a good example of the reverence Greeks have for their old churches. A few blocks west of the cathedral is the Monastiraki quarter, a complex of old houses and shops where the flea market is held daily. Usually teeming with motley crowds, the bustling square is reminiscent of an Eastern marketplace. Huge bunches of shoes, pants, shirts, and other products hang from the doors and windows of stores in the quarter, and salesmen stand in the doorways extolling their wares to passers-by. South of Monastiraki is the Plaka, the entertainment center of Athens. It is the old quarter of the city, full of winding streets, fine old houses, and courtyards filled with flowers. When the Greeks won their freedom from the Turks in 1830, the Plaka was practically all that was left of Athens. Now it is filled with tavernas, *bouzouki* music, and a carnival atmosphere almost every night. In summer many of the tavernas move to the roofs of the buildings, making a walk through the Plaka a colorful and noisy expedition.

Above the Plaka rises the gray and red cliff of the Acropolis, whose crown of broken marble temples is visible from almost any point in Athens. Many ancient cities had an *acropolis* ("highest city") to which the people retreated when attacked, but the Acropolis of Athens was particularly impressive bcause it stood at the very center of the plain around it. At first, the hill was a complete town; then it served as the residence of the kings of Athens. Finally, it became a sanctuary to Athena, the patron goddess of the city in whose honor wooden temples were built on the Sacred Rock. The Persians burned them all in 481 B.C., but during the golden age that followed, the Athenians built magnificent new temples in marble. Today their ruins speak eloquently of the genius that once flourished on the dry plain of Attica.

Millions of words have been written about the Acropolis, and I do not intend to add many more. An appreciation of its temples is essentially an intuitive exercise rather than an intellectual one. While it helps to know something about the store of classical Greek art and architecture on the Sacred Rock, the vision of its temples must be experienced on a personal, emotional level and not with a head full of dates and dimensions. The beauty of these temples will not be augmented by trying to imagine them whole. They possess a new beauty now, different from what they had when they were first built. Conceived as solid forms, they are now mere outlines against the sky. The lines and supple curves that remain, however, create their own rhythms and have a majesty that is all the more effective because the sky can be seen between the columns. The design and construction of the temples was supervised by Phidias, the great sculptor and architect, but the execution was left to other artists. The Propylaea, the entrance, is the work of Mnesicles, who achieved a unity of proportion, despite the difficult site, that impressed even the demanding Athenians of his time. On the bastion to the right stands the exquisite little temple of Athena Nike (Giver of Victory), its narrow Ionic columns made even more delicate by the imposing Doric colonnade of the Propylaea. The Parthenon, the majestic centerpiece of the Acropolis, seems to float at the highest point of the Sacred Rock. This has been achieved by an application of the laws of perspective so sophisticated that succeeding architects have never been able to equal it. The windowless rectangle was designed by the architect Ictinus, who achieved its perfectly linear appearance without using a single straight line, from the slightly convex base to the fluted Doric columns that taper toward the top and lean toward the center.

Just as the temple of Athena Nike offsets the Propylaea, the Doric strength of the Parthenon is balanced by the Ionic grace of the Erechtheum, which stands on an incline to its left. The Erechtheum was built not only in honor of Athena, to whom the Parthenon was dedicated, but also of Poseidon, god of the sea, and of Erechtheus, the deified early king of Athens. The three porticoes of the temple, each on a different level, represent the variety of worship for which it was constructed. The sourthern portico is supported by the famous six caryatids, as sturdy as the strongest columns and as supple as young maidens. One of them is a modern replacement, the original having been taken by Lord Elgin to England along with many sections of the Parthenon's frieze. The others are casts of the originals that have been moved inside the Acropolis museum to prevent further corrosion by air pollution, which has caused more damage in recent years to the marbles of the Acropolis than the destruction of twenty-four centuries.

Every time one sees it, the Acropolis touches the heart in a different way. The mood and color change with the time of day. In early morning the marble columns seem as cool as the skin of a pearl; at noon they seem to pulse under the midday sun; and at sunset they glow gold and red as if lighted by an inner fire. But at night when the moon is full the Acropolis takes on a truly mystical beauty. Everyone who walks up the Sacred Way and sees the forest of ruins shining in the moonlight is filled with a kind of religious awe. Even children become quiet and the place is majestically silent except for the footsteps of ghostly figures gliding in and out of the shadows.

In a corner behind the Parthenon is the Acropolis Museum, sunk below the surface of the Acropolis so as not to intrude on the skyline. Small and beautifully arranged, it contains many of the masterpieces of archaic and classical art that have been found on the Acropolis. The exhibits range from sculptures of ferocious lions battling fierce bulls that survive from early temples on the hill, to statues brilliantly carved by Phidias for the Parthenon.

After seeing the monuments and visiting the museum, one should pause to take in the view of the city below. The Acropolis is high enough so that one can clearly see all that remains of ancient Athens and yet it is low enough so that one can feel the pulse of the modern city. On a field below the northwestern edge of the Sacred Rock lies the *agora*, the center of ancient Athens, where Socrates strolled and Saint Paul preached to crowds assembled in the marketplace. Besides the many ruins, the *agora* is the site of the Stoa of Attalus, which was completely rebuilt by American archaeologists in the Pentelic marble of the original. It now serves as a museum of the *agora*. To the west, on higher ground, is the Temple of Hephaestus, better known as the Theseion because it was long mistaken for a temple dedicated to the legendary king of Athens. The Theseion is the best-preserved Doric temple in Greece, and is a half brother to the Parthenon because of its beauty and harmony.

A short distance beyond the *agora* is the ancient Cerameikos Cemetery, a line of tombs stretching along the road that leads to Eleusis from the Dipylon Gate, which was the main entrance to Athens in ancient times. Traces of the gate, parts of the city wall, and many tombstones can still be seen. The great Panathenaic religious procession formed at the Dipylon Gate, crossed the *agora*, and climbed to the Acropolis. Athenians also gathered at the gates to march along the Sacred Way to Eleusis, where mysterious rites were celebrated. Eleusis today is an industrial suburb of Athens, but the ruins of the sanctuary of Demeter and the site of the Eleusian mysteries are still visible.

The Plaka covers the northern slope of the Acropolis. Wedged into its western end is the Roman *agora*, the center of Athens during the Roman period. Not far off is the Tower of the Winds, so called because of the reliefs relating to the winds that are carved around its top. Actually the tower was a huge hydraulic water clock built in 140 B.C., complete with sundial and weather vane. Across the eastern fringe of the Plaka is the Arch of Hadrian, built by Athenians for the Roman emperor in appreciation of his many contributions to the city. Behind the arch are ruins of the temple of Olympian Zeus, the largest temple ever built in Greece. The Olympeion, with its colossal Corinthian columns, was begun by the Athenian tyrant Pisistratus in the sixth century B.C. and was completed by Hadrian seven hundred years later.

On the southern slope of the Acropolis lie some of the most historic ruins of Athens. Just below the temple of Athena Nike is the restored Odeon of Herodes Atticus, where concerts and ancient Greek plays are staged every summer. The 535-foot-long Stoa of Eumenes, a king of Pergamum, connects the Odeon to the Theater of Dionysus, where the works of Aeschylus, Sophocles, Euripides, and Aristophanes were first performed. Above the *stoa* is the sanctuary of Asclepius, the god of healing, where, in ancient times, water from underground springs was believed to cure illness. Today only fragments of columns remain and the well heads of the springs are bricked over.

Across from the Propylaea are the three famous hills of Athens. Nearest the Acropolis is the rock on which Ares, the god of war, was tried for slaying the son of Poseidon. The site came to be known as the Areopagus—the hill of Ares—and in the time of the Athenian kings men accused of murder were judged there. On the same hill Saint Paul preached his famous sermon about the Unknown God. Slightly behind the Areopagus is Pnyx Hill, once the meeting place of the Athenian people's assembly and now the vantage point for watching the *son et lumière* (sound and light) performances on the Acropolis from April to October. The highest hill is crowned with a marble monument to Philopappus, the Roman consul for whom the hill is named. On its slope is an open-air theater where folk dances are performed during the summer.

The picture of Athens's glorious past that emerges from a tour of its monuments becomes most vivid when coupled with a visit to its best museums. The National Archaeological Museum houses the most comprehensive collection of ancient Greek art in the world. Among the highlights are the Hermes of Andros, the Mourning Athena, the bronze Poseidon, and the golden death mask of Agamemnon. The Byzantine Museum has a superb collection of icons, and the Benaki Museum offers an excellent display of Greek national costumes, jewelry, and handicrafts. The new Goulandris Museum contains a unique collecton of Cycladic art from the islands in the middle of the Aegean. Although these statues were carved five thousand years ago by artists who had no metal tools and rubbed the marble figures with pebbles of emery, their austere, abstract elegance seems as modern as anything found in museums of twentieth-century art.

Despite its rich cultural offerings, the charms of Athens have become tarnished in recent years by the the results of its rapid growth. One of the city's greatest drawbacks is the dark cloud of fumes from the traffic, factories, and refineries that descends periodically like a lid over the city. Greeks call it the *nefos* (cloud), and it rivals even the infamous smog of Los Angeles at its worst. Besides the injury it does to the people of Athens, it is corroding the city's priceless monuments to the point of threatening their existence.

The pollution is one result of the city's massive growth, which has sent its population soaring tenfold since World

War II and has created severe growing pains. Too many vehicles and too narrow streets force motorists and pedestrians to compete fiercely for space. The noise level is usually ear-splitting. The crush of population and tourism has stretched the traditional hospitality and courtesy of the citizens (only those within Athens) to the breaking point. Inadequate city planning has concentrated a majority of the country's manufacturing plants in or near the capital and has produced large tracts of ugly blocks of offices and flimsy apartment buildings where once stood lovely neoclassical mansions. Far too many of the city's architectural beauties have fallen to the demolisher's wrecking ball, and the bucolic charms that delighted Byron have vanished. Gone is the stream that flowed near the Temple of Olympian Zeus that Socrates found "so deliciously cold to the feet," the groves where Plato and Aristotle taught their students, and the open spaces where Athenians through the centuries walked, played, and rested under lofty plane trees.

Despite these unfortunate changes, it is foolish to judge the country by Athens alone, or to allow unpleasant experiences in the city to spoil for one the tranquil beauties that lie a short taxi ride away. Once the major monuments and museums have been visited, excursions outside the city can be a journey back in time to places of pre-industrial serenity and beauty. One of the most rewarding drives is to Cape Sounion, along one of the most beautiful stretches of seacoast in the world. Hardly fifteen minutes from the capital, pastel beaches and iridescent caves beckon travelers to stop for a swim. Sounion itself is a rocky headland 40 miles southeast of Athens, soaring 147 feet above an exquisite bay. On the top is the famous Doric Temple of Poseidon that was built to appease the god of the sea when Athena was chosen instead of him as the patron of Athens. The marble columns rising toward the heavens above the pro-

montory moved even the dour Herman Melville to yield to
the poetic muse:

> Aloof they crown the foreland lone,
>   From aloft they loftier rise—
> Fair columns, in the aureola rolled
>   From sunned Greek seas and skies.
> They wax, sublime to fancy's view,
>   A god-like group against the blue.

The sun setting into the sea behind the temple of Poseidon
is a sight that has tested many gifted poets from Byron (who
scratched his name into one of the columns) to Rilke, but it
still defies description.

Much closer to the city but still by the sea is Piraeus, the
port of Athens. A short subway ride from Omonia Square,
Piraeus has several harbors, the largest of which is quite
near the subway stop. A little farther away are the yacht
harbors of Pashalimani and Tourkolimano, rimmed with
outdoor restaurants where a visitor can choose his dinner
fresh from the sea. When driving to Tourkolimano from
Athens it is worth stopping on top of the Castella hill just
above the harbor to savor the most beautiful view of Athens, all the way from the sea to the mountains, especially
spectacular at night.

The mountains across the plain from Piraeus are almost
as rewarding as the seaside. The mountain nearest Athens
is Hymettus, which is famous for the variety of wild flowers
that grow on its slopes and for the honey produced by bees
that browse on its heather. Kaisariani is an enchanting deserted monastery on the mountain, with a Byzantine
church, the remains of the monastery buildings surrounding
a courtyard, and a fountain that figured in Greek legend for
its ability to ensure fertility.

Even more impressive is the monastery of Daphni, about six miles west of Athens. Its eleventh-century Church of the Assumption is decorated with some of the most brilliant Byzantine mosaics in the world. The monastery itself was built in the sixth century by Justinian, and incorporated materials from the ancient sanctuary of Apollo that stood on the site. Every year in September and October the pleasantly wooded grounds around the monastery are the setting for the Daphni Wine Festival. For a nominal admission charge, visitors can sample as many as seventy wines produced in Greece. The general celebration includes folk dancing, singing, and relaxed dining in open-air restaurants set up especially for the festival. The use of these ancient grounds for a modern bacchanal is indicative of the way Athenians regard their city. They do not look upon it as a sun-drenched museum with nothing to offer but its past. They see it as a city where beauty exists to be enjoyed and where life can be as pleasant today as it was when the marble temples on the Acropolis shone new.

TEN

The Mainland

"Where'er we tread 'tis haunted, holy
ground."
LORD BYRON

From Athens it is possible to drive to almost any part of mainland Greece in a day and to fly to the most distant city in a little over an hour. Yet the face of the country changes so dramatically that a visitor can feel he has seen a hundred worlds and all history come alive. It is possible in some parts of Greece to drive past Doric temples, Roman bridges, Byzantine churches, medieval fortresses, and Turkish minarets in about the time it takes to go to the local shopping center back home. Small though Greece is, it would take months to see all the sights. But it is possible to take in many of the best of them in a relatively short time.

Chief among the areas most worthy of exploration is the Peloponnesus, a hand-shaped land mass connected to the Greek mainland by a bridge spanning the Corinth Canal, a deep channel just broad enough for a single ship. It was completed at the end of the last century, after many unsuccessful attempts had been made to cut a seaway through the narrow isthmus. One of the first was by Nero, who tried to encourage his labor force of Jewish prisoners by digging in person with a golden shovel. Modern Corinth, built in 1928, is of little interest except as a base for excursions. Ancient Corinth lies three miles south of the modern city at the base of the towering mountain fortress of Acrocorinthus. On the summit there now stands a Venetian castle, but in ancient times the mountain was crowned by the Temple of Aphrodite, where a thousand sacred courtesans practiced their art in honor of the goddess of love. With a port on both the Corinthian and Saronic gulfs, ancient Corinth became a wealthy commercial and maritime power. When the Romans conquered the city in 146 B.C., the Corinthians resisted in minor but irritating ways, such as by throwing filth from their windows on to the heads of Roman ambassadors. The Romans exterminated the population, and the city was abandoned for a century until Julius Caesar repopulated it with colonists. In A.D. 51 Saint Paul preached there and reprimanded the Corinthians for their frivolous and dissolute ways. The city was abandoned at the end of the fourth century after numerous attacks by Goths and a series of earthquakes had destroyed large parts of it; most of the ruins that survive today date from the Roman period. The thick, pinkish columns that stand on a rise above the ruins are from the Temple of Apollo built in the sixth century B.C. Also extant is the ancient Pirene fountain, where, according to the ancient myth, the winged horse Pegasus was drinking when Bellerophon caught him.

Southeast of Corinth is the Argolis, a peninsula jutting into the Saronic Gulf that was the setting for some of the most dramatic events in Greek history and legend. The Argolis was one of the earliest inhabited regions of Greece, the first settlers probably arriving as early as 5000 B.C. The most glorious era in the Argolis was the Mycenaean period, from the sixteenth to the twelfth centuries B.C. The palace of Mycenae is some thirty miles south of Corinth, high on a hill overlooking the Argive plain. The walls of the fortress,

from ten to fifty feet thick, are entered through a monolithic
square gateway surmounted by a deeply carved relief showing two lionesses confronting each other. A road wide
enough for chariots leads to the palace at the highest point
of the fort. It was this road, according to the legend, that
Agamemnon traveled on his return from Troy to his death
at the hands of his adulterous wife, Clytemnestra. As described in the first chapter, Mycenae is a haunting citadel,
one of those places in Greece that seizes the imagination
and touches emotions that are deep and powerful. "You
must climb up here to the palace of Agamemnon," wrote
Nikos Kazantzakis after a trip to Mycenae, "in the grip of
wild passion—hate, love, war, terror—in order to see the
Argolid, the mountains and the sea as the Atreids would
have seen them."

At the base of another mountain south of Mycenae is
Argos, one of the earliest cities in Greece. It dominated the
peninsula before the rise of Mycenae and once again in the
twelfth century B.C., when the Dorians conquered the area
and made Argos their base in the eastern Peloponnesus.
During the latter time, it was surpassed in power only by
Sparta. A small town of recent origin lies on the site of the
ancient city, but it is surrounded by ruins of a glorious past,
including an ancient theater of the third century B.C.,
Roman baths, and traces of temples to Apollo and Athena.
Four miles south of Argos stand the ruins of Tyrins, a city
surrounded by thick, rough walls that are said to have been
built by the Cyclopes. According to legend, Tyrins was the
birthplace of Hercules, whose twelve labors were performed
for the king of nearby Mycenae. Tyrins flourished as a Mycenaean satellite until it was destroyed by the Dorians. The
ruins visible today are of an ancient palace with separate
quarters for the king and queen and no connecting door
between them. Under the palace runs a series of secret pas-

sages leading to mysterious vaulted chambers whose purpose has never been explained.

Within sight of Tyrins, on the edge of the sea, stands
one of my favorite places in Greece. It is Nauplia (*Nauplion*
in Greek), the port of ancient Mycenae and the first capital
of modern Greece. Full of narrow streets, Venetian architecture, and pleasant gardens, it is named after Nauplius, the
son of the hero Palamedes, who fought at Agamemnon's
side in Troy. The dramatic cliff that towers over the town
bears the hero's name and is crowned with a massive Venetian fortress that is among the most imposing in the country. The fortress, with its zigzag stairway up the face of the
cliff and its sweeping aqueduct, is a monument to Venetian
mastery of military architecture. The rooms within its ramparts were once used by the Turks as prison cells, one of
which is said to have held Theodoros Kolokotronis, the
bandit leader of the Greek War of Independence. In the
town below, John Capodistria, the first president of Greece,
was assassinated in 1831 as he was leaving a church. Nauplia remained the capital until 1834, when the seat of government was moved to Athens.

Nauplia is a perfect base for touring the Argolis. The
setting is beautiful, the town charming, and it has excellent
hotels. The Xenia is by the sea on a hill below the Palamidi.
It is built at a slight angle so that almost all of the rooms
have a view of both the fortress and the Aegean below.
Some distance beneath the Xenia is the Amphytrion Hotel,
which looks toward the harbor and the Bourdzi, a miniature Venetian stronghold set on an island right in the middle
of the harbor. The stronghold was once used as a home for
retired executioners.

Twenty miles east of Nauplia, in a wooded valley surrounded by mountains, is Epidaurus, the ancient sanctuary
of Asclepius, the god of healing. A child of Apollo and a

Boetian princess, Asclepius was left by his mother on a mountain at Epidaurus to die. He survived, however, suckled by a herd of wild goats, and Epidaurus became a sanctuary to the god. Hordes of pilgrims came there from all over the ancient world to seek the healing powers of Asclepius, and the offerings they left in gratitude enriched the sanctuary. Every four years, a festival was held in honor of the god with games, musical competitions, and theatrical performances. The theater in which the productions were staged was built in the sixth century B.C. on the slope of the mountain where the infant Asclepius was abandoned. The crescent-shaped banks of stone seats rise steeply upward from the circular stage. With the pine-covered mountainside as a background, the enormous 14,500-seat theater is one of the most dramatic sights in Greece. It is also the best preserved theater in the country, and every June and July the works of the classical masters are staged there under the stars. In addition to the theater, there are at the sanctuary the ruins of a stadium, a gymnasium, a temple, and a hotel for pilgrims. But it is not just the ancient monuments that make Epidaurus so commanding. The setting itself is so green and beautiful, the air so clean and pure, that it seems like no other place on earth. "I never knew the meaning of peace until I arrived in Epidaurus," wrote Henry Miller after visiting the sanctuary. "As I entered the still bowl [of the theater], bathed now in a marbled light, I came to a spot in the dead center where the faintest whisper rises like a glad bird and vanishes over the shoulder of the low hill, as the light of a clear day recedes before the velvet black of night. Balboa standing before the peak of Darien could not have known a greater wonder than I at this moment. There was nothing more to conquer: an ocean of peace lay before me."

Deep in the Peloponnesus, southwest of the Argive

plain, two formidable mountains, Parnon and Taygetus, guard the broad Eurotas River valley, where the Dorians established their capital after conquering the Mycenaean empire. Sparta was the city they founded, but it was more a collection of villages than a city, for the Spartans were more interested in war than in architecture. Thucydides noted that future ages would find it unbelievable that Sparta and Athens were once equal rivals, for Athens would leave marble monuments that would endure for centuries but Sparta's wooden buildings would vanish. Indeed little of ancient Sparta remains. The modern city, with its double boulevard and broad square, was built after the War of Independence. The people who settled it came principally from medieval towns built on the edges of the two mountains nearby, and it is these abandoned but amazing strongholds that are worth the drive to Sparta.

The most dramatic of these towns is Mistra, built on a spur of Mt. Taygetus by the Frankish ruler Guillaume de Villehardouin. It is essentially a Byzantine city despite the Frankish castle that dominates it. The red-tiled roofs of Byzantine churches, their stone walls weathered by the sun, rise above narrow winding streets to create a bold pattern of light and shadow. The churches are clustered around three Byzantine monasteries. The walls and domes inside are painted in the late Byzantine style that was to inspire Western art through the works of El Greco.

South of Sparta, on the most easterly of the three peninsulas that jut out from the Peloponnesus, is Monemvasia, the Gibraltar of Greece. Monemvasia is a huge rock that rises out of the sea like a monstrous anvil. On the summit sits a walled Byzantine citadel. The one narrow strip of land left on which to approach the stronghold gave the rock its name: Monemvasia means "single entrance." On a shelf of the rock is a nearly abandoned town whose one main street is a narrow lane that is lit at night by oil lanterns. In the citadel above is a lovely domed and buttressed church, Aghia Sophia (Holy Wisdom), which was built in the thirteenth century.

Northwest of Monemvasia, where Mt. Taygetus thrusts down into the central peninsula of the Peloponnesus, is the remote mountainous region called Mani. Its fiercely independent inhabitants have never allowed any conqueror to subjugate them completely. The Maniots even escaped conversion to Christianity until well into the ninth century. During the Turkish conquest, Greeks from the valley moved up to Mani for the independence its isolation offered them, but these refugees quarreled with the established Maniots, resulting in the formation of constantly warring clans. Rival families barricaded themselves in towers that they secretly extended at night so that they would be in a better position to bombard their enemies the next day. Fine examples of this tower architecture can be seen in the village of Pyrgos Dirou on the western side of the peninsula. Farther north, near the town of Kardamili, is a Frankish fortress spectacularly set between two peaks of Mt. Taygetus.

North of Kardamili lies the Messenian plain, which is as fruitful as any area in Greece. The plain produces the delicious Kalamata olives that take their name from the principal port in the area. The town of Kalamata is beautifully situated around a bay with the peaks of Mt. Taygetus rising in the distance behind it and an excellent beach stretching for miles on its eastern flank. It is a good place to rest on the way to the third peninsula of the Peloponnesus, on whose western shore lies Pylos, one of the world's most striking natural harbors. The wide harbor is protected from the sea by what is actually a long island of rock. But the island is so close to the mainland at its northern end that it looks like a promontory. On its southern end the rock is pierced at several points to form natural gateways to the harbor. On this rock in 425 B.C., four hundred Spartans were trapped by the Athenians for seventy-two days in the Peloponnesian War. Twenty-two centuries later, in 1827, when Pylos was known as Navarino, 26 British, French, and Russian ships defeated 126 Turkish and Egyptian vessels sent to crush the Greeks in their struggle for independence. When the sea is calm, remnants of the Turkish ships can still be seen in the depths of the bay. Pylos is a favorite Peloponnesian resort. On a hill not far from the modern town are the ruins of the ancient city, which was ruled by the wise king Nestor, whom Homer describes as an ally and friend of Agamemnon and Odysseus. It was to Pylos that Telemachus, the son of Odysseus, came in search of his father. Telemachus was royally received in a splendid palace, whose ruins have been partially excavated by archaeologists. They include a throne room, living quarters, baths, and a storeroom where enough utensils were found to equip a banquet for two thousand guests.

Some distance to the northeast of Pylos is Arcadia, the Switzerland of ancient Greece. While wars and revolutions raged throughout the rest of the ancient Greek world, the people of this land lived in peace for centuries. On a small plateau overlooking the tranquil valleys in the heart of Arcadia stands the magnificent Doric Temple of Bassae. Ringed by distant majestic mountains, it magnificently unites the splendor of the Greek landscape with the serene power of Greek architecture. The temple is dedicated to Apollo, but it takes its name from the surrounding region. Designed by Ictinus, one of the architects who created the Parthenon, it is not made of marble like most Greek temples, but of local blue-gray limestone.

In a tranquil and fertile setting fifty miles from Bassae lies Olympia, where the Olympic Games were held every

four years from 776 B.C. to A.D. 392. "In all Greece," wrote
Nikos Kazantzakis, "there is no landscape more inspiring,
none that so gently and perseveringly invites peace and rec-
oncilation. The ancients chose it with unerring eye, so that
every four years all the clans of Greece might gather here,
to sport and to fraternize." During the games, fighting
throughout Greece stopped and athletes from all over the
ancient world gathered at Olympia to participate. The
games lasted for five days and included wrestling; boxing;
foot, horse, and chariot racing; and discus and javelin
throwing. The games were ended when the emperor Theo-
dosius closed down all pagan sites in the fourth century.
They were not revived until 1896.

Olympia was a sacred site long before it became the
setting for the Olympic Games. The prehistoric earth
mother, Gaia, was worshiped there, and Mt. Cronion,
which dominates the area, was consecrated to Cronus, father of Zeus. When the worship of Cronus gave way to the
worship of Zeus, Olympia became the most important sanctuary of the new god. Even more commanding than the
stadium where the games were held was the colossal Temple
of Olympian Zeus, for which the great sculptor Phidias
created a huge ivory and gold statue of the god. The statue
disappeared but the temple lasted until Byzantine times,
when an earthquake shattered it. Only the stumps of the
temple's columns still stand, their drums lying staggered
where they fell, amid weeds and wild flowers. Olympia also
had a temple honoring Zeus's wife, Hera. Although women,
along with slaves and barbarians, were not allowed to participate in, or even watch, the Olympic Games, young maidens competed at Olympia in separate events dedicated to
the goddess. The ruins of Hera's temple still exist, along
with remnants of altars, administrative buildings, gymna-
siums, and treasure houses, the last built by various cities to

hold the offerings left for Zeus after the games. Numerous statues from these structures, as well as the frieze and pediment from the Temple of Zeus, which may be the work of Phidias, are in the Olympia Museum, whose collection of ancient Greek art is surpassed only by those in Athens and Delphi. The most magnificent piece is a beautiful marble statue of Hermes holding the infant Dionysus, which was created by Praxiteles in the fourth century B.C.

Patras, the largest city in the Peloponnesus and the third biggest port in Greece after Piraeus and Thessaloniki, lies directly north of Olympia near the western entrance to the Gulf of Corinth. In classical times the city allied itself with Athens against Sparta and later it flourished under the Romans. Saint Andrew was crucified by the Romans there. The Turks burned Patras during the War of Independence, but it was rebuilt in 1829. The architecture shows a strong Italian influence, and the streets are crowded and colorful. During the fifteen days that precede Orthodox Lent, Patras is the gayest city in Greece. It is a time of continuous carnival featuring masked balls, fireworks, and numerous parades, and Greeks from all over the country visit the city to join in the fun.

The narrow straits leading into the Gulf of Corinth, which are known as the little Dardanelles, are just northeast of Patras. The straits are flanked by two small ports—Rion on the Peloponnesus side and Andirion on the mainland opposite. Ferryboats loaded with cars, trucks, and passengers continually make the fifteen-minute trip across the straits and link western Greece with the highway that crosses the northern Peloponnesus and the Corinth Canal to Athens. The fifteenth-century Castle of Morea at Rion faces the seventeenth-century Castle of Roumeli at Andirrion. A few miles to the east is Naupactus, a small town built around a harbor and enclosed within the horseshoe

walls of a Venetian fort. The Athenians, Spartans, Macedonians, and Romans all fought bloody battles to take and
hold the town because of its strategic importance. But the
most famous battle of all was fought in the sixteenth century when the town was known as Lepanto. In that crucial
naval engagement, the fleet of the Christian powers sank
the greater part of the Turkish fleet and stopped the Ottoman empire from further expansion into Europe. Cervantes,
author of *Don Quixote*, fought at Lepanto and lost the use
of his left hand in the battle.

About twenty-five miles west of Naupactus is Missolonghi, the stronghold of the Greek insurgents in the War of
Independence and the place where Byron died in 1824. Byron's statue dominates the Park of Heroes in Missolonghi
today. The city is at its best at dusk, when the setting sun
gilds the still waters of the lagoon and the scattered islets
around it.

From Missolonghi the highway leads north through tobacco fields and olive groves to Agrinion, the main city in
the Aetolian plain, and then on to Amphilochia, a small
seaside town that is a pleasant place to rest before driving
deep into Epirus. Epirus, which means "continent" in
Greek, is one of the wildest and most beautiful regions in
Greece. Mountains rise out of scrub-covered hills like giant
whales on a choppy sea, then give way to narrow valleys
shaded by plane trees. In spring, columns of shepherds lead
their flocks and families to the high summer pastures as they
did in Homer's time. In the towns and cities skilled crafts-
men work silver and gold jewelry into centuries-old patterns.

Because Epirus is remote, beautiful, and rich in history,
but is almost unknown to the masses of tourists who visit
the country every year, I have decided to devote a separate
chapter to it. The birthplace of Hellenic culture, it has infi-

nite rewards for those willing to explore it and, although I may be accused of prejudice because I was born in the mountains of Epirus, centuries of visitors have fallen under its spell.

The road from Amphilochia to Epirus's capital, Ioannina, runs westward to Igoumenitsa, the port on the Ionian Sea from which ferries leave regularly for Corfu. East of Ioannina a narrow, tortuous road over wild mountain ranges leads from Epirus to Macedonia and beyond to Thrace. The last two regions make up the area known as Northern Greece. Its capital is Salonica (Thessaloniki), the second largest city in modern Greece, which is connected to Athens by a modern highway. Founded in 315 B.C. and named in honor of the sister of Alexander the Great, it enjoyed its greatest prosperity during the Byzantine period, when it was the most important city in the empire after Constantinople. The armies of the Second Crusade occupied it in the twelfth century and in 1430 it was conquered by the Turks, who held it until 1912. Remains from all these periods are scattered amid the blocks of apartment houses and office buildings of the modern city. Near the waterfront stands the Venetian White Tower, built as part of a sea wall in the fifteenth century. Farther inland is the engraved Triumphal Arch erected by the Roman emperor Galerius (A.D. 305–11). Reminders of the Ottoman occupation include a fluted minaret, abandoned baths, and many Turkish houses. Some of the best examples of Greek Christian art can be seen in the half-dozen surviving Byzantine churches. The oldest is the Church of Saint George, a Roman rotunda with a broad dome covered with fine mosaics of the fifth century. Now a museum, it was turned into a mosque by the Turks, and its minaret still stands. Also noteworthy are the small chapel of Saint David, with its fine mosaic of a beardless Christ seen in a vision by the prophets, and the

Basilica of Panayia Acheiropoietos (Our Lady Not Painted by Human Hands), an icon of the Virgin supposed to have been miraculously painted, which once hung in the church. The mosaics in these three churches show classical influences. In the Basilica of Saint Demetrius, the city's patron saint, the Byzantine feeling dominates. One of the finest basilicas in Christendom, it was partially burned in 1917 and restored; its four brilliant mosaics were not damaged. Almost as imposing are the mosaics of the Cathedral of Saint Sophia, a smaller replica of Saint Sophia in Constantinople.

West of Salonica lies the heartland of the rugged region of Macedonia. Pella, capital of the ancient kingdom and birthplace of Alexander the Great, is about twenty-five miles from Salonica. The Romans destroyed it in 168 B.C., but recent excavations have unearthed part of its ruins; the most interesting are the fine pebble mosaics of its courtyards. Edessa, with its many waterfalls, and nearby Naousa, known for its dry white wine, are almost halfway between Salonica and the western border of Macedonia. Set around a peaceful lake to the west is Kastoria, the fur center of Greece, where fur coats can be bought at astonishingly low prices.

Southeast of Salonica is the Chalcidice peninsula, which terminates in three fingers of land extending into the Aegean. On the easternmost finger is Mt. Athos, with its twenty monasteries decorated with frescoes and icons and containing the richest collection of Byzantine records and treasures in the world. The first monastery, Aghia Lavra, was built a thousand years ago, the last, Roussikon (Russian), in the nineteenth century. To visit Mt. Athos and partake of the hospitality provided by the monasteries, it is necessary to get a special permit from the Greek Foreign Office in Athens or from the office of the Governor General in Salonica. Women are barred—indeed no female creature, other than cats and chickens, is allowed on Mt. Athos. The ban was decreed by the founder of the first monastery, Saint Athanasius, in accordance with a rule set down by the founder of his order: "Have no animal of the female sex in domestic use, seeing that ye have renounced the female sex altogether, whether in house or in field, since none of the Holy Fathers had such, nor does nature require them."

Eastward from the Chalcidice peninsula the main road follows a majestic rocky coast. The main town of the area is the port of Kavalla, ancient Neapolis, where Saint Paul once landed. The town, which has some fine beaches nearby, contains excellent examples of Turkish and Egyptian architecture, including the imposing house (complete with elaborate harem quarters) of Mehemet Ali, the Ottoman commander against the Greeks in the War of Independence (mentioned in chapter 5), whose troops occupied Kavalla. Near the town is the site of ancient Philippi, named for Philip of Macedon, the father of Alexander the Great. Here, in 42 B.C., Octavian and Mark Antony defeated Brutus and Cassius, the assassins of Julius Caesar. Among the ruins are a Greek theater, the Roman forum, and an impressive sixth-century Byzantine basilica. From Philippi and Kavala, the road moves across Thrace to Alexandroupolis, the last important town in Greece before the Turkish border. The town was built in 1877 and is not of great historical interest, but it has some excellent beaches and it is a favorite yachting center in the northern Aegean.

Some distance south of Salonica there appears on the horizon the peak of Greece's highest mountain, Olympus, where gods dwelled in splendid palaces fashioned by Hephaestus, the god of fire and metalworking. One has only to look at Olympus rising majestically above the sun-browned earth to realize why the ancient Greeks believed it to be the home of the gods. The mountain marks the northern limit of Thessaly, the largest province in Greece, which occupies most of the central region of the country.

The national highway from Salonica to Athens skirts the eastern end of Mt. Olympus and descends to the city of Larissa, the capital of Thessaly, which is built on the site of several ancient towns. Sixty miles to the west, the little town of Kalambaka crouches at the foot of sheer massive rocks that rise out of the valley like huge stalagmites threatening to pierce the sky. Perched at the top of these rocks are the famous Meteora monasteries, which starting in the four-teenth century were built by monks who found the caves in the Meteora rocks ideal havens from the secular world. Twenty-four monasteries were ultimately finished; all but five are now abandoned. Two of them offer accommoda-tion for visitors, and all contain fine Byzantine frescoes. "The rocks of Meteora," Baron Houghton wrote after vis-iting the monasteries in 1832, "are perhaps the most mar-velous combinations of Nature and Art, of the strange humors of geology and humanity, that the world presents."

South of Larissa, the highway passes Volos, a pleasant seaside town with a wide harbor. Near the entrance to the town are the ruins of ancient Iolcus, the city in which Jason organized the Argonaut expedition. In Lamia, a town set between two pine-covered hills, some sixty-five miles far-ther south, a medieval fortress crowns one hill and a tourist pavilion the other. Both offer marvelous views of the city below and the countryside around it.

From Lamia a road leads east through the narrows of Thermopylae, where Leonidas and his three hundred Spar-tans fought to the death against the invading Persians in 480 B.C. Coastal silting has widened the pass to a broad plain, but the site of the battle is marked by a towering statue of Leonidas flanked by three hundred cy-press trees. On the base of the statue is written Simonides' epitaph:

Go tell the Spartans, thou who passest by,
that here obedient to their laws we lie.

The air around Thermopylae has an acrid smell, and steam
can sometimes be seen rising out of the ground near the
road. The volcanic nature of the land suggested by these
phenomena is soon confirmed when the road leads to Kammena Vourla, a fashionable health spa built around highly
radioactive springs. Near Kammena Vourla is the famous
Spring of Aphrodite, where the chloride and hydrogen sul-
fide content of the water has made it sought after for centuries as a complexion treatment.

From Kammena Vourla the highway follows the coast
and then curves inland past the outskirts of Thebes (Thivai
in Greek). According to myth, the ancient city was founded
by Cadmus, who came from Phoenicia in search of his sister, Europa, after she was carried off by Zeus. One of Cadmus's successors was the tormented Oedipus, whose fate is
one of the most powerful themes of Greek tragedy. The
Thebans enjoyed a brief period of supremacy in Greece after
defeating the Spartans, but they in turn were crushed in 338
B.C. by Philip of Macedon. The Theban dead from this
battle were buried in a collective grave, above which was
erected the statue of a lion. The statue still stands in Chae-
ronea, some distance west of modern Thebes. The town
itself has little to show for its glorious past besides the ruins
of a palace built during the late Mycenaean period. Not
far away is the monastery of Ossios Loukas (Holy Luke),
built for a local saint who lived nine centuries after the
author of the gospel. The monastery complex constructed
around the crypt where the saint is buried contains some
fine frescoes and the best mosaics in all of Greece. North
of Ossios Loukas, the road climbs higher and higher and
then cuts cleanly across the foothills of Mt. Parnassus. On

a natural throne just above the road is the Oracle of Delphi.

Enough has been said about Delphi in the first chapter. The ancient oracle seems an appropriate place to end our journey of the most dramatic sites in Greece. As pointed out earlier, the setting at Delphi is so compelling that god and man could hardly have resisted pausing here to talk. The beauty of the site itself was not enough for the Greeks, however, for they had no hand in its creation. They added temples, theater, treasure houses, all of such quality that they enhanced the natural beauty around them.

This is what stands out in any journey through Greece. Wherever nature distinguishes itself—at Athens, Sounion, Epidaurus, Mistra, Olympia, Dodona, Mt. Athos, Meteora, Delphi—Greeks have not stood in awe or moved in clumsily. Instead they have tried to find the best in themselves to create monuments worthy of their land. The wonder of it is that they have succeeded so often and so well.

ELEVEN

Epirus –
The Genesis
of Greece

"On Souli's rock and Parga's shore,
Exists the remnants of a line
Such as the Doric mothers bore."
LORD BYRON

L ord Byron first stepped on to Greek soil in the
remote, nearly unknown province of Epirus in
1809 and fell instantly under the spell of its stark mountain
scenery, inhabited by colorful nomadic tribes and steeped
in history. It was while visiting the court of the notorious
Turkish ruler Ali Pasha in Ioannina that Byron began the
epic *Childe Harold*, which would bring fame both to the
unconventional young poet and to the isolated province,
enticing such notables as Gladstone and Disraeli to venture
into its wilderness. Like many travelers before and since,
Byron believed that no other part of Greece could match
these towering peaks and steep ravines where "roams the
wolf, the eagle whets his beak, birds, beasts of prey and
wilder men appear."

I was born near the top of one of those mountains of
Epirus in 1939 near the Albanian border. Nine years later,
I left my village for the first time with three of my sisters in
a night escape planned by our mother, Eleni, to save us from
being abducted with the other village children behind the
Iron Curtain by the Communist guerrillas who had occu-

pied our village during the Greek civil war. At the last moment, my mother was prevented from going with us, drafted for a work detail. As she said goodbye, she warned us to throw a black stone behind us when we left, a charm to insure that we would never return. She was thinking of the famine, war and hardship that had plagued our mountains for the past decade. We left the stone, but the vow not to return was one I couldn't keep, for, as I wrote in the book *Eleni*, "The isolation and cruelty of the landscape made the peasants short-tempered and sometimes drove them mad . . . but those who managed to escape from these mountains would never find any other place as beautiful."

I returned to Epirus and my village of Lia fourteen years later, at the age of twenty-three, and have been back nearly every year since. Until 1974, Lia was still in the "forbidden zone"—so close to Albania that a special pass was needed to enter. Plumbing was unknown, electricity was a novelty, the single road was unpaved. (Almost half the Epirus that Byron visited is still inaccessible because it fell inside Albania when the boundary with Greece was arbitrarily set by a commission in 1923. The current rulers of Albania won't let anyone in or out.)

Today the harshness of life is only a memory, although mountain goats still leap on the vertiginous cliffs and wild boar dig ruts in the high plateaus with their snouts. In Lia, there is not only plumbing but a small hotel, with a bathroom for each of its ten rooms. Civilization, in the form of the great homogenizer, television, has invaded the most isolated corners of Epirus, but for the evanescent present, the province still offers scenes that would have been familiar to Byron or even Olympias, the mother of Alexander the Great, who was born here: mountain pastures dotted with flocks of goats and sheep watched over by grizzled shepherds in the same rough hooded capotes admired by Byron;

black-kerchiefed women spinning raw wool on their hand-carved distaffs or bent nearly double under towering piles of kindling. In Ioannina, the capital of the region, where Byron was entranced with the Arabian Nights splendor of Ali Pasha's court, storks still nest atop minarets inside the ancient walled city and peasant women in native costume sell produce in the teeming outdoor market. In the nearly alpine scenery of Metsovo, bearded men wearing their black kilts, pillbox hats, and homespun leggings gather daily in the square to play backgammon while the women, in bright hand-woven skirts and embroidered aprons, sit at their looms in the front windows.

Nowhere else can you find as much evidence of all phases of Greece's history. The mystic Acheron of mythology, the river the ancient Greeks believed flowed to the nether world, runs through the region. Dodona, the ancient oracle of Zeus, fourteen miles from Ioannina, predates Homer, who mentioned it in both the *Iliad* and the *Odyssey*. Monuments of the powerful Molossian tribes that produced both the mother of Alexander the Great and King Pyrrhus who so nearly defeated the Romans in battle, are all over the region, including my own village. The ruins of Nikopolis, built by Octavian to celebrate his victory over Antony and Cleopatra, dominate the plain near the bay of Actium where the naval battle was fought. Churches and monasteries throughout the area offer a spectacular panorama of Byzantine architectural styles and Ioannina is one of the few areas in Greece where evidence of the four hundred years of Turkish occupation has not been obliterated.

In my own village of Lia, scarcely a pinprick on the the map of Greece, it's hard to plow a field or dig a cellar without stumbling over the relics of the Hellenes and invaders who have passed this way. When the Germans burned

my grandfather's house in 1944, he dug a new foundation
and unearthed a Roman sword that now rests in my office.
At the top of our mountain, above the timberline, an ancient Hellenistic acropolis stands sentinel. It belonged to the
Molossian empire, four centuries before Christ, and formed
a link in the chain of fortresses stretching from the seaport
of Chimara (now in Albania), to the ancient site of Dodona.
Signal fires could be seen from one acropolis to the next—
a pre-Christian telegraph system. When I was a child, the
local storytellers peopled the acropolis above our village
with medusas and chimeras, minotaurs and griffins—fan-
tastic creatures passed down by oral tradition by hundreds
of generations of peasants who knew nothing of books and
history. Oddly, the inhabitants of my village still refer to a
plateau near the acropolis as the "Agora"—the ancient
Greek word for "marketplace"—even though no one passes
through it but wild boar and the occasional shepherd. The
atavistic memory of pagan rituals is still woven into the
daily life of the Epirots. In many villages, they put coins on
the eyes of corpses before burial as the ancients did to pay
the way to Charon. The survivors dig up the bones of the
dead several years later and wash them in wine—just as
wine stains were found on the bones in the tomb of Philip
of Macedon at Vergina. Every year on July 20th, our villagers climb to the highest peak to light fires to the prophet
Elias near his small white chapel. They have no idea that
this is a Christianized version of the worship of the sun god
Helios, whose temples were rebaptized in the name of the
prophet. Fires have been lit on this peak to pray for good
weather and crops since time immemorial.

The mountains of Epiros, my mountains, have been
trampled by every invader of Greece—Crusaders, Bulgars,
Slavs, Romans—and the inhabitants have for centuries
withdrawn into their caves and fortresses in an attempt to

save themselves. My mother nursed me in the caves above our village while hiding from the invading Italians in 1940. Generations before, the villagers hid in the same caves from the Turks. The Ottoman empire held Epirus captive for 482 years, from 1431 to 1913, and their minarets and the sign of the crescent can still be found. My father left Lia in 1910 wearing the red fez and pantaloons of the Turkish overlords. His first gesture on boarding the steamer for the United States was to throw the fez into the sea. Until his death in 1983 at the age of ninety-two, he liked to chuckle over the passport that listed his nationality as Turkish.

My village is in the part of Epirus called Thesprotia. According to Aristotle, it is here that the Greek race began and the Greek language first took shape. So isolated are the people of our mountains that intermarriage has preserved the fair coloring, blue eyes and classical Greek features of Pericles' time as nowhere else. Byron's observations about the people of the region are not entirely inappropriate today: "They are cruel, though not treacherous, and have several vices, but no meannesses. They are, perhaps, the most beautiful race, in point of countenance, in the world; their women are sometimes handsome also, but they are treated like slaves, beaten, and in short complete beasts of burden."

Europeans generally enter mainland Greece at Igoumen-itsa, the port where ferries from Corfu and Brindisi dock: a bustling but unprepossessing seaport lined with souvenir shops hoping to lure the tourists before they board buses, cars, or rented motorbikes and set out on the mountain roads toward Ioannina. There is little to charm a visitor into lingering at Igoumenitsa except the prospect of good swimming and the evening promenade along the quay, but when I first entered it in 1948, the sleepy fishing village seemed a metropolis to me.

It was here that my sisters and I were housed in corru-
gated tin shacks (most of them now vanished) in a large
refugee camp. We cooked at an outdoor fire, used the ravines for a bathroom, screened our living quarters from the
others with a hanging sheet. I squandered nearly all my
refugee allotment on a huge box of Turkish Delight, resulting in a memorable stomach-ache. But the most vivid memory of Igoumenitsa was my first sight of the sea—an
incredible prospect for a child who had always lived on a
mountaintop. I plunged into the surf, convinced it would
buoy me up, and I would have drowned if some local boys
hadn't contemptuously pulled me out, laughing all the while
at my hand-knit underwear.

The winding road from Igoumenitsa leads over the
mountains to Ioannina, the capital of Epirus, which my
sisters and I visited shortly after escaping from our village.
The shock of entering my first city is still vivid. I gaped at
the shop windows, the storks and minarets and ancient
walls, the beggars and peddlers selling every kind of marvel,
the oriental-style bazaar, the crowds of soldiers and curious
civilians who stared at us escapees from Communist territory. A sympathetic bystander bought me an ice-cream
cone. Never having eaten anything frozen, I dropped it at
the first taste, crying that it had burned my tongue. Today
vendors still sell ice cream, nothing special by Western stan-
dards, but my children consider it worth the trip. Ioannina
is the most picturesque and unspoiled large city in Greece.
Today, as in the days of Ali Pasha, storks fly over the walled
Turkish city with its minarets, tiny cobblestoned streets,
baths, and fortresses. It also contains a synagogue built in
1790, one of the four that once served the large Jewish
community. The Turks were driven out in 1913, and the
Jewish population was rounded up and shipped off to concentration camps in 1944, but the signs of their culture
abound and the city still maintains an Oriental flavor.

Byron was fascinated with the rich panoply of the court of Ali Pasha in Ioannina and quickly adapted the gold-embroidered native costumes. He wrote about the exotic appearance of the Albanians, Tartars, and Turks, the magnificent palaces ("splendid, but too much ornamented with silk and gold"). The silver and gold filigree work that charmed the style-conscious Englishman is still a specialty of the area. Gold is a bargain in Ioannina and many famous jewelers, including the founder of the house of Bulgari, who went on to Rome to make his fortune, learned their trade in this region. Byron wrote to his mother that he was graciously received by the great Turkish ruler Ali Pasha ("one of the most powerful men in the Ottoman empire"), but he was well aware of the Pasha's reputation as one of the most brutal despots of his time: "He has the appearance of anything but his real character, for he is a remorseless tyrant, guilty of the most horrible cruelties."

Ali Pasha ransacked Epirus for Greek youths for his Janissary Corps and pretty girls for his harem, which included as many as five hundred concubines. His seraglio of young boys occupied his time equally. Any subjects who displeased him were tied in sacks and thrown into the mirrorlike lake that surrounds Ioannina on three sides. Today the ghosts of the drowned concubines hover over the lake in the morning mists, and at sunset the water reflects the minarets of the Turks' past glory as the citizens embark on the evening stroll from the central square in front of the town hall, down past the walled city to the lake side, where outdoor cafés and restaurants, and in summer, carnival rides and shadow puppet shows, abound. Ferries dart back and forth to the island in the center where Ali Pasha met his death at the hands of one of the sultan's emissaries (the spot is now a museum) and where can be found some of the best outdoor restaurants serving frog legs, crayfish, eels, and freshwater trout pulled fresh from the lake.

About three miles out of the city is the hill of Perama hiding one of the most dramatic stalactite caves in Europe. A well-lit concrete path meanders through the whole cave to an exit at the opposite end, making it possible to explore the whole forest of stalactites and stalagmites without retracing any steps.

Some forty-two miles (sixty-eight kilometers) northwest of Ioannina is my birthplace, Lia, perched high on the Mourgana mountain range near the Albanian border. Now a sleepy village of 180, it once boasted 750 people, three gristmills, and eleven churches. The ordeals of World War II and the subsequent civil war left it virtually deserted, and only a handful of the old people filtered back to scratch a living out of the soil. The younger Liotes who survived the war and the Communist occupation preferred, like most of their fellow Greeks, to head for the cities where life had more to offer.

But lately, like most villages in Greece, Lia has been showing unexpected signs of revival. While two-thirds of the stone houses in Lia are in ruins, overgrown with vines, a score of new homes have been built there and more are started every year. Greeks, young and old, are taking a new look back at the village life that they left so eagerly. The urban areas, crowded far beyond their capacity, have fallen victim to acute air pollution, crippling traffic jams, and inadequate sewage, mass transit, and educational facilities. "The smoke, the traffic, the rat-race in Athens, they kill you before your time," says Athanasios Bartzokis, former mayor of Lia. "Here, the old people live into their nineties. Climbing up and down the mountain slopes gives you a heart like iron."

But life in villages like Lia is hardly a pastoral dream. Less than a generation ago, most of the inhabitants hovered on the edge of malnutrition, surviving on beans and mountain greens and eating meat only a few times a year. Better days and the arrival of modern civilization were signaled by the completion of a road in 1959, connecting the village to the outside world. Electricity came in 1965, and candlelight and traditional folk songs were supplanted by an electric bulb hanging in each room and radios that blared forth popular music from Athens. Television quickly followed, and though only one channel can be received in Lia, inhabitants in homespun black cloth quickly learned how the rest of the world dressed, spoke, and thought, absorbing "Kojak" and "Dallas" along with advertisements for such conveniences as refrigerators and washing machines. Four years ago, Lia had only one telephone—a hand-cranked model in the village coffee shop, which worked for a few hours each day—and no bathrooms. Today the bathrooms number three dozen, and there are eight telephones. "Lia has much to offer—the best hunting in Northern Greece, the purest water, spectacular views, traditional skills in handworking brass and copper. There's even an acropolis above the village dating back to 300 B.C.," says Antonis Venetis, a lawyer who heads the Athens fraternal order of Liotes. "But until recently, there was no one left in the village except old people waiting to die."

Although the Greek government has provided limited funds for reviving its villages, many communities are trying to initiate projects on their own, tapping the fierce love that even expatriate Greeks have for the villages where they were born. Former inhabitants of Lia who have traveled to Athens and even to the United States have joined in an attempt to raise enough money to build a small inn and hunting lodge that would accommodate about twenty guests as well as a restaurant and a store selling handicrafts. So now Lia not only has television and telephones but also tourists, and ambitions of becoming a small version of Metsovo, a prosperous mountain village one hundred miles to the southeast, which reversed the exodus of its inhabitants by restoring the ancient homes and reviving its traditional crafts of wood carving, cheese making, and weaving.

Metsovo, hidden in the snow-covered peaks of the Pindus mountains where it nestles among forests of firs, provides an authentic glimpse into a part of Greece's past never pictured on the travel posters. Cut off from the rich plains of eastern Greece by a breathtaking pass called "Katara" ("The Curse"), it is a lovely time capsule, looking more Swiss than Greek. It includes a ski jump and chalets, cheese and woodworking factories, and produces the best red wine in the country.

Metsovo is preserved as it was in its glory. Its wealth resulted from a special dispensation from Turkish taxes and restrictions because a peasant from the town gave sanctuary for a year to a Turkish vizier, in disgrace with his sultan, who promised on his return to power to grant him any wish. As a result of its special privileges, Metsovo attracted many rich Christian families who built magnificent walled mansions, designed to be self-sufficient during the harsh winters and attacks from marauding brigands. The Museum of Metsovo is the completely restored mansion of the local titled family called Tositsa. It has the stables, storerooms, and fountains within the building's walls on the first floor, and on higher floors the winter and summer bedrooms, grilles through which the secluded women could watch the comings and goings of visitors, rooms for cooking, weaving, listening to musicians, or attending to business, all filled with the rugs and tapestries, handicrafts, arms, silver and gold, and carvings for which the region was famous; even the wardrobes are full of the richly embroidered garments that designated the status of the wearer.

Most inhabitants of the town wear the colorful old hand-woven costumes and practice the ancient crafts of embroidery, wood carving, weaving, and cooking just as they did centuries ago. But unlike the inhabitants of Williamsburg or Sturbridge Village, the Metsovites are not play acting but stay in costume twenty-four hours a day. Their old ways never died, but were researched, encouraged, and revived by the government and descendants of the town's renowned philanthropists, including the Averoff-Tositsa family.

The citizens of Metsovo, who belong to a people called the Vlachs, speak not only Greek but also their own language, which, like Romanian, is descended from Latin. The ancient crafts, skills, beliefs, even recipes, have been rescued from oblivion by Evangelos Averoff, one of Greece's leading political figures, and his nephew, a former mayor of Metsovo, Yiannis Averoff. Yiannis's wife Elena, who speaks a dozen languages, is a fountain of information about the history of the region. The Averoff family has also restored several old churches and chapels in the area, with priceless icons, carvings, and altar screens.

I remember fondly an Easter I spent in Metsovo as their guest when Yianni was mayor. As the citizens of Metsovo gathered in the churchyard at midnight on Holy Saturday to wait for the Resurrection, an unseasonal snow fell silently over the churchyard and towering fir trees, creating a Christmas-card-like setting. The next day, as was the custom, the entire populace filed through the Averoffs' beautifully restored home—Elena was wearing her native costume heavy with chains of gold sovereigns and Turkish piastres. They gave each of their constituents a red Greek Easter egg and portion of the seven lambs that had been roasted in the cellar.

Most visitors to Epirus never suspect the existence of

Metsovo, a medieval world off toward the east, but instead they head from Ioannina southward toward Athens. On the way they may stop for a visit at the ruins of Dodona, the most ancient oracle in Greece, compared to which Delphi is an upstart. Dodona was old when Ulysses went there to cleanse himself after murdering Penelope's suitors, and is referred to in the *Iliad*, the *Odyssey*, and the works of Herodotus. The priests were called Helloi, from whom the Greeks—who refer to themselves as Hellenes and to their country as Hellas—got their name, according to some historians. In a state of inspired frenzy, the priests interpreted the words of Zeus in the rustling leaves of the sacred oak. The Argonauts were said to have a piece of wood from this tree fitted into the keel of the Argo, enabling the ship itself to speak at critical moments. After I first visited Dodona in 1963, I could no longer scoff at such legends. As an evening breeze swept through the trees that stood like sentinels around the temples and echoed against the sheer stone cliffs of Mt. Tomaros, I could easily understand how the rustling leaves of a giant oak were accepted by my ancestors as the voice of God.

Thirty miles from Ioannina, on the road to Athens, travelers must choose either the western branch, leading to Nikopolis, Preveza, and Actium, or the eastern branch to Arta. Both routes are rewarding. The eastern road passes through the sleepy town of Arta, surrounded by orange groves, which was twice the capital of Epirus. On the site of the ancient capital of King Pyrrhus, Arta reached its zenith in the thirteenth century when some of the most magnificent Byzantine churches in Greece were built there. It is now best known in folk songs, especially for its graceful arched bridge, which still stands. According to legend, when the bridge was being built, the arches would collapse every day:

The builders lamented and the apprentices wept,
"Alas for our toil, pity for our labors,
   all day we build, at night [the bridge] falls!"
A little bird passed and alighted across the river,
   it didn't sing like bird or swallow,
   it sang with human voice and said,
"Unless a human life is given, the bridge will not stand;
   nor must you sacrifice an orphan, a stranger, or a
     passer-by,
but only the master-builder's beautiful wife,
who comes late in the morning and very late in the
   afternoon."

The master-builder heard and was saddened unto
   death;
he sent a message to his beloved by the nightingale:
"Dress slowly, get ready slowly, come late in the
   afternoon,
slowly walk and come across to Arta's bridge."
But the bird did not heed and went and said
   differently:
"Dress quickly, get ready quickly, come quickly at
   noon,
quickly walk and come across to Arta's bridge."

There she came walking down the white road,
The master-builder saw her and it broke his heart.

She was lured onto the spot and as she realized she was
being buried alive, she placed a curse on the bridge. Eventually the chief mason committed suicide.

   The ruins of Nikopolis, on the route to Preveza, are all
that remain of the cosmopolitan city founded by Octavian
to commemorate his victory at Actium, "where once was

lost a world for woman," as Byron wrote. Here, when it had a population of 200,000, Saint Paul preached and wrote his Epistle to Titus and the philosopher Epictetus had his school. Today the ruins stand like gravestones, as the hawks wheel overhead.

Beyond the ruins of Nikopolis lies Preveza, on the Ambracian gulf—where Byron first entered Greece. The site was founded by Pyrrhus, occupied by the Venetians, ceded to the Turks and then to the French, and retaken by Ali Pasha. Now, amid olive groves and orchards of lemon and orange trees, it provides travelers a pleasant respite by the sea: modest seafood restaurants, a colorful evening promenade, quiet swimming, and a look into the heart of Greek life without the intrusion of foreign tourists. Although not rich in Byzantine architecture like Arta, ancient remains like Dodona, or oriental atmosphere like Ioannina, Preveza offers a magnificent view of the distant boundaries of Epirus to the visitor who stops and looks back at this neglected part of Greece. "The dark mountains of Souli and the snow-carpeted summits of more distant Pindus," wrote Dr. Henry Holland from here in 1815, "form one of the most magnificent backgrounds the imagination can offer." Those mountains were peopled during the long Turkish occupation by fierce fighters who lived free of Ottoman control until 1803, when they were surrounded by Ali Pasha's army. As the Turks moved in, sixty women escaped with their children to a mountain summit, where, after performing their ritual dance, they threw their children over the precipice and then jumped into the chasm after them rather than become slaves of the enemy.

On the coast west of Souli lies Parga, one of the most beautiful seaport towns in all Greece and the last Christian stronghold in Epirus to fall to Islam. In 1817 the British, who were in control, sold it to Ali Pasha. Taking the icons from their churches and their ancestors' bones from their tombs, the Parquinots sailed away to Corfu. They got a measure of revenge against the Turks in the Greek revolt that broke out a few years later, however, when a native of Parga, Constantine Kanaris, destroyed much of the Turkish fleet by sailing small boats close to the enemy's frigates under cover of night, setting them on fire just before jumping off, and letting them smash into larger Turkish warships. Some natives of Parga returned to the town over the years, but the icons were not brought back until Epirus was finally freed from the Turks in 1913.

Like Antaeus, who would weaken and die when not touching the earth, most Epirotes, however far we are scattered, feel a need to return to the soil that bore us. Every Greek goes home to his village, if only in his thoughts, on its name day. My village, Lia, celebrates its annual festival on Saint Elias's day, July 20. Emigrants come from as far away as Australia and the United States and climb the highest peak to worship at the prophet's chapel, then descend to the *agora* below the ruined acropolis to dance, eat, and drink in festivities that last for three days. I knew my birthday was in July, but it wasn't until 1963 that I learned the actual date. An old woman in the village recalled how, on the third day of the prophet's festival, July 23, 1939, my mother sent for the midwife and I was born—the long-awaited son—setting off more days of feasting and celebration.

I'm glad that black stone we threw behind us in 1948 failed in its spell. Nowhere else do I have such a sense of place, such a feeling of being part of the continuum of life. Nowhere else but in Epirus would my birth be remembered in connection with a festival that has been celebrated since the natives worshiped the ancient sun god. The first thing one Greek asks another upon meeting is the name of his region, because the place of one's origin explains so much. Harsh as the region may be, I expect to go back to those mountains for as long as I can climb them and, each time, to draw new strength from the soil of Epirus.

TWELVE

The Islands

"All are living still, the islands, mothers of heroes. Flowering from year to year. . . ."
FRIEDRICH HÖLDERLIN

The islands of Greece shine like fragments of an ancient mosaic in the Ionian Sea to the west and in the Aegean to the east of the mainland. To visit them is to come closest to the pulse of Greece. There is no single island culture. One island may be a bustling harbor filled with stevedores and ships; another may be a chic, sundrenched gathering place for artists, painters, and wealthy shipowners; another may be a barren rock inhabited by fishermen wresting a bare living from the sea; still another may be an ancient city of narrow winding streets, horse-drawn carriages, and Old World charm. But the blue-green water surrounding every Greek island seems to have protected them from the pressures, materialism, and neuroses of modern civilization. The island Greeks are the easiest to get to know. Just sit at a harborside café watching the fishermen mending their nets, the sailors unloading cargo onto waiting donkeys, the housewives in their black kerchiefs doing their shopping. You will soon be caught up in the island's rhythm and you will wonder if you might not have slipped into a past century.

There are more than 1,400 islands in Greece, but only 166 of them are officially classified as "inhabited." Of these, only about one-third have permanent communities of any significance. In the summer months, their sea-tempered coolness and easy informality make them a haven not only for tourists but also for Greeks escaping the heat of the mainland. In the other months of the year, however, the climate on the islands can range from brisk to cold; the boat, which provides the only link to civilization, comes less and less often, and life can be hard indeed. When Greek islands are mentioned, most people think of the ones spread like steppingstones on the Aegean Sea between the Greek mainland and Turkey. The Ionian islands are often ignored, probably because they are on the opposite side of the country from Athens. But if such an astute judge of beauty as the late Aristotle Onassis picked an Ionian island on which to build his paradise, they too deserve our attention.

Corfu (Kerkyra in Greek), the northernmost of the Ionian group, lies along the southern coast of Albania and the northern coast of Epirus. Poets ranging from Homer, who made it the kingdom of the gentle Phaeacians in the *Odyssey*, to Lawrence Durrell, who lived on Corfu for several years, have celebrated the luxuriant beauty of the island. Homer marveled at its fruitfulness: "Pear follows pear, apple after apple grows, fig after fig, and grape yields grape again." The Turks never conquered the Ionian islands; Corfu's conquerors were all Europeans. It passed through Venetian, French, Russian, and British hands before becoming part of Greece in 1864. Each nation added something to beautify the island's capital (also called Corfu), giving it the unique cosmopolitan ambiance it has today. The Venetians left the massive citadel that dominates the harbor. Within the town, the British built a Regency palace, and the French constructed a replica of half of Paris's Rue de Rivoli, complete to the lamps on the arcaded buildings and the French outdoor cafés on the square. "I doubt if there is any little town as elegantly beautiful in the whole of Greece," wrote Lawrence Durrell.

Although many Greeks consider Corfu too European, they flock to it for its natural beauty and to worship its adopted saint—Spyridon, a third-century bishop who lived in Cyprus. His corpse was carried from Cyprus to Constantinople and finally to Corfu to escape the advancing Turks. Today, it rests in a bejeweled silver casket in a sixteenth-century church, except when it is carried in the four annual processions that celebrate the saint's miraculous intervention in times of epidemics, famine, and siege. Royalty has been seduced by the beauty of Corfu for centuries. The Greek royal family used to spend summers here, and in the last century, the Empress Elizabeth of Austria built a lavish palace called the Achillion, which is a monument to bad taste and nineteenth-century sentimentality. She filled the grounds with statues of Achilles, Greek philosophers, and, incongruously, a bust of Shakespeare. Kaiser Wilhelm II, who found it very much to his taste, bought the palace from Elizabeth's heirs. After World War I no one knew what to do with the disintegrating palace until, in 1962, Baron von Richthofen turned it into a baroque casino, with a hotel on the grounds. The northern terrace is dominated by an immense statue of Achilles and commands a magnificent view all the way to the mountain peaks of Albania. The view alone is worth a visit to the palace.

The more remote countryside of Corfu contrasts strikingly with the cosmopolitanism of the city. The traveler will pass groves of grotesquely gnarled olive trees and sleepy villages of houses painted in pastel washes of gold, lavender, blue, pink, and white that seem almost to vibrate in the sun. Black-robed, bearded priests ride by perched on donkeys,

and peasant women walk along the roads balancing huge
jugs of water on a ring of cloth on their heads. Corfu has
some of the most beautiful natural beaches in the world,
but they are all some distance from the town, and the clusters of hotels around them have diminished much of their
charm. The most famous are at Palocastritsa, where the
shipwrecked Odysseus allegedly was washed up and discovered by Nausicaa. Three bays in the form of a clover are cut
into sheer cliffs and rimmed with beaches of smooth white
pebbles. Enterprising owners of small outboard motorboats
are eager to whisk visitors from the main beach to tiny,
isolated beaches, and then return to pick them up at the
appointed time. Alternatively, they will give guided tours of
the rainbow-hued sea caves in the cliffs. (Be sure to set a
price with the navigator *before* embarking on such a voy-
age, which I failed to do.) At the edge of the main beach, a
restaurant overhanging the water serves lobsters that diners
select from crates suspended in the sea. A winding road
leads from the beach to a lovely thirteenth-century monastery perched on the cliff above. There the monks will show
visitors who are dressed with appropriate modesty some
rare icons and the huge, fossilized bones of a "sea monster."
They may even offer some of the grapes that hang in thick
clusters from the arbors within the monastery.

South of Corfu, in a crooked line, lie Paxos, Lefkas,
Cephalonia, Ithaca, and Zakynthos, which is also known as
Zante. All of them show evidence of their prolonged contact
with European conquerors. Paxos, thirty-five miles south of
Corfu, is a perfect spot for solitary hiking, camping, swim-
ming, fishing, and skin diving in unspoiled surroundings.
Antony and Cleopatra had a feast here on the eve of the
battle at nearby Actium in which they lost everything.

Lefkas, which is separated from the mainland only by a
narrow canal, is bigger and livelier, with an annual festival

of art and literature. On its southern tip, a white cliff that
was originally topped by a temple to Apollo rises abruptly
from the sea. Criminals could prove their innocence by surviving a leap from the summit into the sea; it is said that the
famous Lesbian poetess Sappho, while in a disconsolate
mood, leaped to her death here in the eighth century B.C.
Cephalonia, the largest Ionian island, is crossed by an imposing chain of mountains. Among the ruins on the island
are a deserted Venetian city, tumble-down British barracks,
and a necropolis of eighty-three Mycenaean tombs.

Like Corfu, Cephalonia is rich in verdant hills, spacious
bays, and irresistible beaches, but both the landscape and
the people have a rougher edge to them than those of the
more famous island. Ithaca, just to the northeast, was the
kingdom of Odysseus, Homer's wily hero. The waters from
the spring of Arethusa still flow through the majestic landscape just as Homer described it, and stalactites still hang
above the altar in the Grotto of the Nymphs. In the last
century, Heinrich Schliemann, carried away by his previous
successes at Troy and Mycenae, identified some ruins as
Odysseus's Castle, and the name stuck, even though it was
later proved to be a temple built five hundred years after
the Trojan War. The island's association with Odysseus has
made it a symbol for a man's longing for home, roots, identity, adventure. In his poem *Ithaka*, C. P. Cavafy writes:

> Setting out on the voyage to Ithaka
> You must pray that the way be long,
> Full of adventures and experiences.
> The Laistrygonians, and the Kyklopes,
> Angry Poseidon,—don't be afraid of them;
> You will never find such things on your way,
> If only your thoughts be high, and a select
> Emotion touch your spirit and your body.

The Laistrygonians, the Kyklopes,
Poseidon raging—you will never meet them,
Unless you carry them with you in your soul,
Unless your soul raises them up before you.

Zante, to the south, is an island of gardens and orchards, music and poetry. The Venetians who ruled it for
four centuries named it the Flower of the Levant, and the
graceful arcades they built still stand in the town. Itinerant
musicians play haunting mandolin serenades on the waterfront and the islanders delight in pageantry and church festivals. Dionysios Solomos, the poet who wrote the Greek
national anthem, was born in Zante, and here the Ionian
school of painting flowered. The beaches of Zante are
equaled only by those of Corfu.

Most of the inhabited Aegean islands are divided into
four groups: the Saronic, the Sporades, the Cyclades, and
the Dodecanese. Each group and each individual island has
its own color and character. Some are lush and inviting, but
many are bleak and barren. Some are as lively and cosmopolitan as Syntagma Square; others are as peaceful as Mt.
Athos. But all of them can claim the brilliant Aegean, tur-
quoise and transparent in the shallows, dark and mysterious
in its depths.

Closest to Athens and easiest to reach are the four islands in the Saronic Gulf between Attica and the Peloponnesus. The largest is Aegina, visible from Athens, where a
city of traders flourished more than two centuries before
Christ. Today visitors travel through vineyards and pista-
chio plantations to visit ancient Christian churches and
Doric temples, especially the Temple of Athena Aphaea,
built in the fifth century B.C.

When a ship approaches Poros, to the south, it sails up
a narrow canal, and passengers find themselves staring

straight into the eyes of villagers leaning out of the upper stories of the pink, white and yellow houses. Not far away, a grove of thousands of lemon trees perfumes the air. The ruins of a temple to Poseidon and an Orthodox monastery are the only sites to tempt visitors away from the many fine beaches.

Hydra, just south of Poros, is two hours by boat from Athens, but it seems to be another world. Hydra was settled by stern and independent Greeks from Epirus when they fled the Turkish invasions of the fifteenth century. The island was so poor, especially in water resources, that the Turks did not even bother to tax it, and the Hydriots were allowed to manage their own affairs like a small, independent republic. They turned to the sea, and a few families became wealthy shipowners. The island built up a substantial merchant fleet, willing to take any risk for a price. When the Greeks finally revolted against the Turks, the Hydriots provided a ready-made navy, and the rich ship owning families poured their entire fortunes into the War of Independence. Today many of the magnificent homes on Hydra have been turned into museums. The port of Hydra forms a crescent, and the town rises steeply from the harbor like a natural amphitheater. The buildings are white, with the roofs tiled in the red clay of Greece, and they crowd upon each other like steps in a staircase. Fishermen mend their nets on the quayside while donkeys, the only "vehicles" allowed on the island, pick their way through the tourists, carrying cargo from the ships. Stylish boutiques, full of native wares, line the harbor, including one floating shop installed in a ship that resembles an ancient trireme. There is a strong French influence in Hydra, and the cosmopolitan ambiance of the island, coupled with the low cost of living, has attracted many young people, who fill the harbor with chitchat in a multitude of languages.

Spetsai, the southernmost island in the Saronic chain, also has a seafaring tradition. The ancients called it the "pine-clad" island, and its pine forests still scent the bracing air. Bouboulina, the heroine of the War of Independence, who commanded her ship *Agamemnon* in many engagements against the Turks, was born on Spetsai in a house that still stands. Horse-drawn carriages are the main mode of transportation. The harbor is ringed with gay and colorful cafés that are especially lively during the hours of the traditional evening stroll. Spetsai, Hydra, and Poros are all convenient jumping-off places for a visit to the Peloponnesus and the Argolis.

North of Attica is Euboea, a large island so close to the mainland that is usually considered a part of it. The capital, Chalcis, is at the spot closest to the mainland; an iron bridge spans the channel.

The Sporades, north of Euboea, are among the most beautiful and least known islands in the Aegean. Skiathos has a great many unspoiled beaches—most famous is Koukounaries. With its golden sands fringed by tall pine trees, it is perhaps the finest beach in Greece. It is inhabited mostly by sailors, and its many charms and its low cost of living are luring more and more tourists.

An hour's boat ride to the east lies Skopelos, a reef-enclosed island of great beauty. The student of icons will find Skopelos a paradise, thanks to its 360 churches, 12 convents from the seventeenth and eighteenth centuries (which provide lodging for travelers), and numerous chapels and monasteries. The churches contain vivid frescoes and brilliantly carved altar screens as well.

The largest of the Sporades islands, Skyros, is as rich in history as it is beautiful. Theseus, the founder of Athens, was exiled to the island and died there. According to legend, Achilles was hidden there by his mother in an attempt to protect him from his tragic destiny at Troy. The grave of Rupert Brooke, the English poet who died on his way to Gallipoli during World War I, is on the island. The natives of Skyros are known throughout the Mediterranean for their exquisitely carved wooden furniture, based on designs handed down from the Byzantine period. The island produces a rare breed of miniature horses that can still be seen treading wheat on circular threshing floors as they did in ancient times.

The Cyclades are so called because the large group of islands comprising them seem to form a circle (*cyklos* in Greek) around the sacred island of Delos. The Cyclades are generally barren and rocky but nonetheless striking with their clusters of square white houses shimmering in the Aegean sun. At the center is Delos, according to myth the island on which Leto, pregnant by Zeus and pursued by his jealous wife, Hera, took refuge to bear Apollo, the sun god, and his twin, Artemis. Delos, therefore, became the holiest shrine of Apollo. It was so sacred that when any of the inhabitants were about to die or give birth, they were moved to the nearby island of Reneia. Its only permanent inhabitants today are the custodians of its abandoned cities and shrines. The ruins lie on a field below Mt. Kynthos, whose summit offers a breathtaking view of the sea and surrounding islands. The most impressive ruin is the terrace of archaic stone lions, long and lean as greyhounds, roaring at the sun. Nearby are the remains of three temples of Apollo and, on the slope of the mountain, a number of elegant houses with fine mosaic floors ring the ruins of an ancient theater.

To many visitors, Mykonos, just east of Delos, is the archetypal Greek island. Tourism has brought a bustling new life to this barren rock. The principal attractions are its proximity to Delos, its views of the ever-changing Aegean, and its famous architecture. Centuries ago, the inhabitants of the island created a cubistic style of architecture, using native granite, rubble, and limestone. The buildings on Mykonos are now considered the finest examples of the so-called Cyclades style. The islanders have a passion for cleanliness and whitewash their homes, streets, churches, and stairways over and over again, until the town seems to be built of sugar cubes. Indeed, the buildings gleam with such a whiteness that even on the darkest night one can find one's way without a light around the narrow winding streets. The domes of the hundreds of churches provide a contrast to the "modern" cubism of the houses. Some say that there is a church for every three families on Mykonos; others claim that there are as many churches as there are days in the year. Many squat, white windmills with thatched roofs are visible above the town on the hill. On windy days their white sails wail a lament for the sailors that have gone to sea. Mykonos also offers a wide variety of native crafts, including hand-woven fabrics of unusual design. It is not surprising that so many thousands of tourists every year find Mykonos one of the most pleasant stops in Greece, and pose for a snapshot with the famous pelican that stalks around the harbor with great self-importance. It has attracted a colony of foreigners—artists, writers, and other free spirits—and some visitors complain that this worldly influx has spoiled the primitive charms of the island.

Tenos, to the northeast of Mykonos, is spread around the waterfront and crowned by the Church of Panaghia Evanghilistria. The church houses an icon of the Virgin, which is believed to have miraculous powers of healing. A narrow channel separates the northern tip of Tenos from the island of Andros, the most verdant of the Cyclades group. Until it was pillaged by the Romans in the second century B.C., Andros flourished and produced some fine works of art, including the Hermes of Andros now in the National Archaeological Museum in Athens. During the Middle Ages, a silk industry developed there and the island thrived again. Today it is known for its good beaches, pleasant groves, lively folk festivals, and successful shipping families.

Another home of wealthy shipowners is Syros. Before the Corinth Canal made Piraeus so important, Syros was the major port in Greece and the center of the Greek shipping industry. The wealthy old families, who have been in shipping so long that they consider Aristotle Onassis and Stavros Niarchos upstarts, remember Syros fondly and maintain spacious villas and lush gardens there. Hermoupolis, the main town and the capital of the Cyclades, reflects Syros's prosperous past. Its many large neoclassical buildings are a sharp contrast to the small, whitewashed structures on most of the Cyclades.

South of Syros lies Paros and its tiny sister island, Antiparos. In ancient times, Paros was famous for its white marble, which was used to face the Temple of Delphi. Today, Paros is known to Greeks for the triple Church of Our Lady of the Hundred Gates in Parekia, the main town. Naxos, just east of Paros, is the largest and one of the most beautiful islands of the Cyclades. In the vast open interior are a number of Byzantine churches and a Byzantine castle with excellent frescoes still well preserved. According to myth, it was at Naxos that Theseus abandoned Ariadne, the daughter of King Minos, after she had helped him find his way out of the Labyrinth.

Melos, southwest of Naxos and Paros, is the most historic of all the Cyclades. Excavations have unearthed settlements centuries older than the Minoan civilization, and even today the island continues to yield valuable archaeological finds. The most famous discovery on the island was, of course, the Venus de Milo, which is now in the Louvre. Some distance east of the island is Ios, the home of Homer's mother and probably the site of his tomb. Beautiful and unspoiled, the island has some twenty-five miles of sandy shoreline.

To the south is the volcanic island of Santorini, or Thera. The worst eruption occurred in 1500 B.C.; the latest in 1956, when all but one building in Phira, the capital, was destroyed. The town was rebuilt as it was, on the rim of the volcano, nine hundred feet above the sea. A monastery of the Prophet Elias crowns the mountain, and on the southern slope are the ruins of the ancient city of Thera with its Doric and Egyptian temples and homes. Directly below is the village of Perissa, which borders a black volcanic beach. The bottom drops off so abruptly that one can dive directly into the sea from the sand.

Off the coast of Asia Minor, southeast of the Cyclades, are the Dodecanese (Twelve Islands). The group got its name in ancient times when only a dozen of the more than two hundred islands in the area were inhabited. Today there are permanent communities on fourteen islands, the most important of which are Rhodes, Kos, Kalymnos, Leros, Simi, and Patmos.

Rhodes is the queen of the Dodecanese—the largest, the loveliest, and the most important island in the group. Rich and green with oleander, hibiscus, and bougainvillea in bloom everywhere, the island is drenched in sun almost the year round. Rhodes, however, is distinguished as much for its history as for its climate. Once a commercial empire that rivaled Athens in its prosperity, it later became a center of learning where important Romans, including Julius Caesar and Marc Antony, went to finish their education.

The ancient city, built in the fifth century B.C., was de-

signed by the Miletian architect Hippodamus and was
known for its exquisite beauty throughout the Greek world.
The geographer Strabo wrote of it: "Harbor, roads, walls
and other buildings so much surpass other cities that we
know of none equal, much less superior to it." Straddling
the harbor was the Colossus of Rhodes, one of the Seven
Wonders of the ancient world. A 105-foot-tall bronze
statue of the sun god, Helios, the main deity of the island,
it took twelve years to build. It guarded the harbor for only
fifty-six years before being toppled by an earthquake in 227
B.C. Its ruins remained on the island for another nine centuries until the Saracens finally sold it for scrap. The Jewish
contractor who bought it used 980 camels to carry it away.

Little of the ancient city survives today. The character
of Rhodes is medieval, reflecting the island's occupation
between 1310 and 1512 by the Order of Saint John. The
order consisted of knights, priests, and serving brothers
(hospitalers) subdivided by nationality and ruled by a
Grand Master elected for life. The medieval walled town
dominates the modern city. The town, with its wide ramparts, narrow streets, and inns and lodges, was restored by
the Italians, who ruled Rhodes from 1912 to 1945. The
largest building is the palace of the Grand Master, near the
cloistered hospital of the order. The hospital has been converted into a museum that contains archaeological finds
from Mycenaean to Roman times, including the "Bashful
Aphrodite" of the third century B.C. The modern capital lies
along Mandraki harbor outside the walls of the medieval
town. Built by the Italians during their generation-long occupation, the sea front includes a long, colonnaded administrative building designed in the style of the Doge's Palace
in Venice.

Outside the capital are three dozen villages. Also on the
island are the sites of the three ancient cities that flourished

before uniting into a single republic called Rhodes in order to compete more effectively with Athens and Sparta. The three cities were Kamiros, located deep in the valley of the island, Jalysos on its mountain, and Lindos near its widest bay. In ancient times the acropolis at Lindos was second only to that of Athens. It was dominated by a series of temples to Athena Lindia, the last of which was built in the third century B.C. Sitting at one of the restaurants by the beach at Lindos, it is possible to see a panorama of Greek history in one view: windsurfers sailing in the bay, the traditional whitewashed homes of the village above it, the walls of the medieval fortress circling the hill above the village, and the ruins of the ancient temples on top of the hill. It is one of the most dramatic sights in Greece.

The most northerly of the Dodecanese is Patmos, the Biblical island as sacred to Greeks today as Delos was in ancient times. In the first century, John the Evangelist came to Patmos seeking refuge from Roman persecution. He lived in a grotto there for sixteen months, during which time he received the Revelation and wrote the Apocalypse. Near the grotto, the Monastery of Saint John was established in the eleventh century by a monk who found that "sterile and dreary Patmos" fitted his ascetic nature. The monastery, with its fortress-like walls, contains some priceless Christian treasures, including a partial manuscript of the Gospel of Saint Mark.

Between Rhodes and Patmos lie Simi, Leros, and Kalymnos, the homes of Greece's famous sponge fishermen, who have carried their trade as far west as Florida and South America. Kalymnos, one of the loveliest of the Dodecanese, holds spirited festivals shortly after Easter, when the sponge fishermen begin their five-month voyages through the Mediterranean, and in early autumn when they return home.

Kos was the birthplace of Hippocrates, the father of medicine. In a square in the main town stands a 2,000-year-old plane tree under which Hippocrates is said to have examined patients, and nearby are the springs from which he drew medicinal waters. The island also has many ancient ruins, early Christian churches, Byzantine monuments, a Turkish mosque, and a medieval palace built by the Knights of Saint John. Many isolated beaches rim small coves along the indented coastline.

North of the Dodecanese are a number of islands that do not belong to any of the four Aegean groups. The largest is Lesbos, known in Greek by the name of its capital, Mytilene. Its many beaches, inlets, grottoes, and forests have made the island increasingly popular with visitors, and a growing artists' colony has been established at Methymna, thirty-five miles from the capital. It is appropriate that artists should find the island congenial because Lesbos was the home of Sappho, the greatest poetess of the ancient world, and Aesop, the celebrated teller of fables. The beauty and charm of the island's women predate the poetry of Sappho. Homer describes in the *Iliad* how Agamemnon tried to persuade Achilles to rejoin the war against the Trojans by offering him seven women from Lesbos "who won the chief renown for beauty from their whole fair sex . . . ." The earliest annual beauty contest was held on the island in a temple dedicated to Hera, the wife of Zeus. The poet Alcaeus, a contemporary of Sappho, describes this contest where girls from the island "go to and fro with trailing robes, being judged for beauty, while the marvelous sound of the loud cries of women echoes round them every year."

North of Lesbos is Samothrace, whose mountains soar higher than those of any island in Greece. Its rugged landscape and lack of a harbor have always given it a mysterious, forbidding countenance. In antiquity, the cult of the

Cabeiri flourished on the island. Little is known about them except that they were fertility gods whose chief symbol was a phallus. The parents of Alexander the Great, Philip of Macedon and Olympias, were initiates but the rites were kept strictly secret. The sanctuary where they were held lies near the town of Palaeopolis, which is also close to the spot where the famous Winged Victory of Samothrace, now in the Louvre, was discovered.

Furthest north in the Aegean is Thasos, whose natural beauty can match that of any island in the Mediterranean. The richly wooded slopes of the mountain range that dominates the island fall abruptly along the eastern coast, cutting breathtaking coves and bays in the shoreline. The port of Limin, about an hour and a half from Kavalla by boat, is built on the site of an ancient city. Thasos is rich in archaeological sites because its extensive deposits of gold and silver in ancient times drew settlers from all over the civilized world. Today it is the favorite retreat of Greeks living in eastern Macedonia and Thrace.

On the opposite end of the Aegean is Crete, the largest and most important of the Greek islands. The highest of the mountains that dominate its landscape is Mt. Ida, which rises seventy-five hundred feet above the sea. It was here, according to myth, that Zeus came to die, and the peak of Mt. Ida is said to be an outline of his profile. The people of Crete are dour but brave, and they have given Greece some of its most brilliant men. Eleutherios Venizelos, the great Greek statesman, was born on the island, as was Domenicos Theotokopoulos, better known as El Greco, and Nikos Kazantzakis, the greatest of modern Greek writers.

In the Christian era, Crete came under the rule of the Byzantines, the Saracens, the Venetians, and finally the Turks, who held the island from 1669 to 1898. Evidence of some of these occupations can be seen in Crete's four largest

cities—Heraklion, Chania, Rethymnon, and Aghios Nikolaos—all of which are on the island's northern coast. Heraklion, the biggest city, was heavily bombed during World
War II and rebuilt in a rather nondescript manner, but its
Venetian bastions still dominate the port. A short distance
from Heraklion lie the ruins of Knossos, the center of the
magnificent Minoan civilization that flourished in the Mediterranean from 2200 to 1600 B.C. The city was unearthed
by Sir Arthur Evans, the British archaeologist, who spent
more than $1 million of his own money on the undertaking.
The Palace of Knossos, with its thick columns tapered
downward and its highly advanced plumbing system, was
drastically restored by Evans to offer a dramatic, if some-
what theatrical, picture of the seat of Minoan power and
culture. Its intricate layout explains why some people think
that it may have been the Labyrinth described in the legend
of Theseus. The gay and colorful frescoes that once decorated the rooms of the palace are the outstanding attraction
of Knossos. Among the scenes portrayed in the frescoes is
the death-defying sport of bull-vaulting, in which young
men and women performed acrobatic feats on the horns
and backs of running bulls. Some of the paintings have been
restored and can be seen in the palace and in the Archaeological Museum at Heraklion. The museum also contains a
magnificent collection of Minoan art, jewelry, and delicate
figurines, including two tiny snake goddesses from Knossos.
In the south of the island are the ruins of Phaestos. The
palace there is smaller than that of Knossos, but it seems
more dramatic because of the grandeur of its setting on the
leveled summit of a hill in the beautiful Messara plain with
Mt. Ida rising behind.

In Chania, formerly the capital of Crete, the crowded
old Venetian town surrounds the harbor and is in turn en-
circled by wide roads, green parks, and recent buildings of

the modern city. Between it and Heraklion is the third city of Crete—Rethymnon, which still retains the strong Turkish flavor of old Crete, for its tall minarets rise like spears above the narrow streets.

Behind Rethymnon tower the snow-capped peaks of the imposing White Mountains (Lefka Ori). Overlooking a valley at the foot of the mountains is the monastery of Arkadi, the national shrine of Crete. During the uprising of 1866, several thousand Turks surrounded five hundred Greeks in the monastery. The Greeks vowed never to surrender and when the Turks broke in, the abbot set fire to the powder magazine, killing all but one of the defenders and twenty-five hundred of the enemy. Aghios Nikolaos, some forty miles east of Heraklion, on the shores of the Gulf of Mirabella, is a modern seaside resort with good beaches nearby. To the west is the plain of Lasithi, where eleven thousand iron-skeleton windmills pump up precious water for irrigation.

Cretans are proud of the many famous men their land has produced. Among those buried in their native soil are Eleutherios Venizelos, whose grave is on a small promontory just outside of Chania, and Nikos Kazantzakis, whose body lies under a stone slab in the Venetian ramparts at Heraklion. His epitaph is, in many ways, a motto for all the people of Crete, who have battled cruel enemies and the harsh land throughout their history. It reads: "I hope for nothing. I fear nothing. I am free."

THIRTEEN

Oinoussai—
The Isle
of
Fortune

"And every time, it is ships, it is ships."
D. H. LAWRENCE
The Greeks Are Coming

Far from mainland Greece, Oinoussai is a tiny island, six miles long and less than two miles wide, huddled precariously on the eastern edge of the Aegean within sight of Turkey. For most of its history, it was inhabited only by goats and a few shepherds who lived in constant fear of pirate raids. Today, the small town that clings to the hillside around the harbor has a population of about four hundred. The inhabitants bring in most of the necessities of life by boat from nearby Chios and then use donkeys to carry them up the steps of the winding streets.

Oinoussai might be indistinguishable from dozens of other remote Greek islands except that it has produced an extraordinary crop—scores of fabulously wealthy Greek shipping families including the richest Greek shipowner of them all. Greek shipowners control the largest merchant fleet in the world—70 million tons, which is almost as much as that of all Common Market countries combined. This floating empire is ruled primarily by 180 Greek shipping families, and one-third of them come from Oinoussai, which is the smallest of the five islands that have given

217

Greece most of its shipping magnates. (The others are Cephalonia, Andros, Syros, and Chios.) The richest Greek shipowner in the world is not Stavros Niarchos, Christina
Onassis, or George Livanos, but an Oinoussian named
Costa Lemos. His fellow shipowners sometimes refer to him
behind his back as "Goldfinger," perhaps because of a physical resemblance to the portly fictional villain, but more
likely because his vast fortune in ships, real estate, and in-
vestments is said to exceed $5 billion.

Although they are the least well known, the Oinoussians are considered the most cunning and astute of the
shipping Greeks. Starting with fourteen Liberty ships
bought from the U.S. government after World War II, they
have built a fleet totaling more than five hundred vessels.

Following the war there was a tremendous boom in
shipping, and the Oinoussians seized every opportunity to
cash in on it. During the Korean War, most U.S. merchant
ships were used to transport war materials, leaving international shipping to foreigners. The shortage of ships in an
expanding market sent freight rates soaring. It was possible
to pay off mortgages on new ships after just a few voyages,
and the Oinoussians, always a thrifty lot, had the cash available for down payments on plenty of ships. The recessions
that followed the booms have not hurt most Oinoussians as
much as other shipowners. The key to successful shipping
is to have enough ships on charter in bad times to protect
yourself and enough ships free in good times to clean up
on the high rates. Oinoussians seem to manage this juggling
act better than anyone else. Many of them somehow
anticipated the current decline in international shipping and
quietly sold some of their ships, while putting others on
long-term charters when freight rates were high. "They
know their business. No Oinoussian shipowner I can recall
has ever gone bankrupt," says George Paraskevopoulos, a
maritime lawyer in Pireaus.

The millionaire sons of Oinoussai do not live on the island year round, but almost all maintain homes there and every summer they converge on the island from New York, London, Paris, Geneva, and Athens. Their yachts float like swans in the small harbor, and their villas, surrounded by stone walls, come alive. The two cafés are thronged with customers and the harborside becomes a promenade for women in French *couturier* gowns and children speaking in the accents of English and American boarding schools. In winter, however, Oinoussai has little to attract visitors. The water of the harbor becomes a metallic gray and an icy wind whistles through the empty windows of the hundreds of deserted houses. (In its heyday, Oinoussai's population was 5,000.)

I heard constantly about the Oinoussians in late 1973 while traveling through Europe to research a novel about Greek shipowners. In London, Paris, and Geneva, other Greek shipowners told me numerous anecdotes about the Oinoussians—most of them rather unflattering. One story that frequently came up was meant to reflect on their lack of social polish. It concerned the wealthy Oinoussian ship-owner's wife, recently arrived in London, who carefully studied the fine points of etiquette. When her chauffeur-driven limousine dropped her every Sunday at Saint Sophia, the Greek Orthodox Cathedral on Moscow Road in Bays-water, she was dressed like all the other shipowners' wives in a mink coat and white gloves. But when her husband presented her with a diamond ring of dazzling size and splendor, she was in a quandary. She knew gloves must be worn to church, but then how could the other wives see her magnificent ring? The next Sunday she arrived at Saint So-phia with a hole cut in the finger of her glove, through which the diamond protruded.

Although most such stories are apocryphal, they reflect the attitude of the other shipowners toward Oinoussians,

who are regarded by many of their colleagues with a mixture of scorn and envy. On my first visit I arrived on the
island, like everyone else who doesn't have his own yacht,
on the daily ferry from Chios. As I was watching the
shadow of Oinoussai loom up in the distance, I was joined
at the rail by the boat's owner, a retired sea captain who
bears one of the more prominent island surnames—Lemos.
Like all Greeks, Captain Theodoros Lemos is a philosopher.
He is also a naturalist and a poet as well as the captain of
the ferry and the most enthusiastic dancer in the Aegean
islands. We began theorizing about what makes Oinoussai
unique among the hundreds of Greek islands. Suddenly
Captain Theodoros disappeared below, returning with a
piece of granite in his hand. In the cleft of the rock was a
small mound of what appeared to be dried sandy clay and
perched on top of it was a black bee, which he assured me
was dead. "Only in Oinoussai will you find this bee," he
said, "because only in Oinoussai is life so hard that the bees
must make their honey on the rocks. But their honey is the
sweetest of all." Captain Theodoros insisted that I take the
rock as a gift, complete with the bee that had become stuck
in the clay and died. Then he went to the wheel to steer the
ship into port.

Like the Oinoussian bees, the native shipowners are a
tough, independent breed. Instead of absorbing "jet set"
values, they tend to keep to themselves, marrying within
their own community, avoiding publicity and holding tight
to the island values of a strict morality, religious piety, and
family loyalty. Other shipping families with names like Em-
biricos, Goulandris, Livanos, Carras, and Nomikos, who
come from other islands, have assimilated more easily into
the society of the European cities where they maintain
homes and offices. But the Oinoussians, through they often
live abroad, carry on their island traditions. Every Christ-

mas, for instance, special bread that has been blessed in the Church of Saint Nicholas on Oinoussai is distributed to the homes of Oinoussian shipowners, be they in London, Paris, Geneva, or Athens.

Unlike many of the shipowners from other islands, the Oinoussians, when they have made their fortunes, rarely take to collecting works of art, race horses, or soccer teams. Instead they concentrate their energies on their families, their ships, and their native island. Their patriotism, however, sometimes tends to be a little flamboyant. When Strovili Lemos built himself a home in North London costing millions, in addition to a chapel, five marble bathrooms, and separate nurseries for boys and girls, it also included a swimming pool made in the shape of the island of Oinoussai. Even more striking is a small islet, in the center of the harbor of Oinoussai, which belongs to a shipowner named Stefanos N. Pateras. He has had it built up on either end so that it looks like a huge ship with the word PATERONISO (Pateras island) emblazoned on the side in giant letters so that it is clearly legible to every resident of the town. On top of the "ship" is a whitewashed chapel and a family villa.

The love of Oinoussai permeates every level of the shipowners' lives. At an elegant name-day party I attended in Athens for one of the young sons of a shipping family, a cousin of Costa Lemos, Leon Lemos, made a speech. After some congratulatory remarks he began scolding the assembled shipowners, all Oinoussians, for not being generous enough to their *patrida*—fatherland. "It is the fault of our wives," he thundered. "Instead of asking us for mink coats, they should ask us to give the money to our fatherland." Only after he had spoken for several minutes did I realize that the man was not referring to Greece, as I had first assumed. By *patrida* he meant the island of Oinoussai.

Most of the sixty shipping families of Oinoussai belong

to about half a dozen clans, and their family trees are inter-twined into a true Gordian knot. The Oinoussians have intermarried so extensively that nearly everyone is everyone else's cousin. One shipowner named John Hadjipateras, for example, married a distant cousin, Maro Pateras, whose sister later married John's nephew. Now John is his neph-ew's brother-in-law and Maro is her sister's aunt. Wealthi-est of the Oinoussian dynasties is the Lemos clan. They number around twenty-five families who own 250 ships. Foremost among them, of course, is Costa Lemos—the richest Greek shipowner of all. Although his name is scarcely a household word, Costa Lemos has consistently managed to out-guess, out-maneuver, and out-class his more well-known rivals. According to those who know him, he has all the qualities attributed to the better known "golden Greeks"—decisiveness, imagination, and dedica-tion to work. But Lemos knows ships better, because, like all the Oinoussians, he grew up in shipping. After getting a law degree, he spent seven years on ships, earning both an engineer's and a captain's ticket. Onassis, on the other hand, made his money in tobacco and then bought ships with it, while Niarchos's family owned flour mills in Ath-ens, which gave him his start.

Costa Lemos is also legendary for paying attention to the smallest detail of every one of his ships. Captain Theo-doros Lemos spent twenty-five years working on Oinous-sian vessels, but he says he would never captain a ship belonging to his kinsman Costa Lemos. "A captain on a Lemos ship can't even buy a case of Coca-Cola without authorization," he says. Another quality that tends to put Costa Lemos ahead of the other shipowners is that when things look most hopeless, he tends to find a new and orig-inal solution. Many men might have become discouraged if, like Lemos, they had lost every ship in World War II, but

Lemos took the one Liberty ship he was allowed to buy from the U.S. government and with it began to rebuild his massive shipping empire. While his competitors waited anxiously after World War II for overbooked European shipyards to get to their orders, he went to Japan and found that shipyards there could build good ships much faster and cheaper than those in Europe. By the time other shipowners got over their prejudices about ships "made in Japan," Lemos's ships were already sliding down the shipways.

Personally Costa Lemos is a mystery, even to his fellow Oinoussians. He has returned to his native island only once in fifteen years and unlike the other shipowners has not donated to it any public edifices bearing his name. Perhaps this accounts for the fact that native Oinoussians have sometimes been less than complimentary about their compatriot. (Lemos did, however, contribute $4 million to Greece in 1974 during the country's confrontation with Turkey. Most Oinoussians and the majority of other shipowners also made contributions.)

Costa Lemos has two sisters and a brother, Adamantios. His relations with his sisters are extremely close. (His sister Maria is the widow of John P. Goulandris of the prominent shipping family from Andros, and mother of Peter Goulandris, the man Aristotle Onassis, on his deathbed, reportedly asked his daughter to marry.) But Lemos was estranged from his brother for many years because Adamantios married a Greek woman of whom his father Michalis did not approve. The two brothers have since become reconciled. In 1948, Costa was married to Evi Dambassis, the daughter of a shipowner from Andros, but the marriage did not work out, nor did it produce any heirs. Three years after it was dissolved, Costa married a young woman from his own island, Melpomene Pateras. She was twenty years younger than Costa. Some shipowners who know the pair claim that Costa decided on her before he met her, simply on the basis of her picture.

His second wife soon provided him with three children, two girls and a boy, who will inherit their father's dozens of companies in as many countries, including a 31-story apartment block at 1041 Third Avenue, which houses the New York headquarters of Lemos's "Triton Shipping Company." Although he has offices in several countries, his main headquarters, C. M. Lemos & Co., Ltd, is in London.

Lemos and his family live in Lausanne, Switzerland, and there is apparently nothing about his life, public or private, that would excite public interest. Unlike Onassis, who would dine at restaurants like "21" where he often ran into journalists and photographers, Lemos selects restaurants like the Coach House in New York and the White Tower in London that are good, expensive, and quiet. Whatever city he is in, he makes it a point to attend church every Sunday. "What Costa Lemos prays for is more ships," say his detractors. But Lemos is unlikely to want more ships, at least at present. Like all big shipowners, he has had to lay up some of the ships he already owns because of the current slump and to sell a number of others.

Another branch of the Lemos family, one that has been constantly involved in the civic affairs of Oinoussai, was headed for many years by Andreas G. Lemos, a lawyer as well as a shipowner. Andreas Lemos wrote many books and pamphlets recording the maritime history of Greece and especially of Oinoussai. Like his five brothers, he earned his master's certificate and, like so many Oinoussians, he saw the sea claim many members of his family, including a grandfather, a brother, three uncles, a brother-in-law, and three nephews.

Even more common than "Lemos" in Oinoussai is the name "Pateras." There are actually three separate Pateras clans and the name "Pateras" is the one most frequently seen on public buildings and monuments. One prominent branch of the Pateras family is descended from Ioannis C. Pateras, born in 1829, who captained a Turkish ship when Oinoussai was still under Ottoman rule. Ioannis had three daughters and three sons. One of his sons, Konstantine, traveled to Jerusalem to visit the Holy Sepulcher, a pilgrimage that entitled him to change his name to Hadjipateras, launching still another branch of the family. Konstantine's brother, Diamantis, had six sons, all of whom became multimillionaire shipowners. When one son, Panagos Pateras, died of a type of cancer known as Hodgkin's disease in 1965, it set off a bizarre chain of events that momentarily turned the spotlight of publicity on an aspect of Oinoussian life that shipowners rarely discuss—their religious beliefs.

Panagos Pateras was married to an attractive daughter of the equally prominent Lemos clan. Katingo Pateras was as sophisticated as any shipowner's wife—at home in half a dozen cities and several languages. She had three children, two girls and a boy. Her youngest child, Irene, was born in 1939. Irene was very beautiful, and as she grew up she led the life of a typical shipowner's daughter—skiing in Gstaad, crossing the Atlantic with her parents on the Queen Elizabeth, vacationing on the Greek islands. But Irene demonstrated early an extremely pious bent. According to a Greek Orthodox priest who knew her, "She was the most spiritually advanced young person I have every met."

In the 1940s the stocky, mustached Panagos Pateras discovered that he was suffering from Hodgkin's disease. However, the cancer went into remission, and then, in 1959, young Irene contracted Hodgkin's disease as well. Family friends say she had prayed to take on her father's disease and after she came down with it, his appeared to subside. Before her death, Irene's religious feelings became

even more intense and she decided to become a nun. Although she had the best medical treatment, she died in her
twentieth year and received the stark burial that is given to
Greek Orthodox nuns and monks—she was put directly in
the ground, wrapped in a shroud, without even a wooden
coffin. Overwhelmed with grief, her mother began to build
a convent on one of the breathtaking cliffs of Oinoussai, far
from the settled part of the island. She called it Evangelismos (Annunciation), and spared no expense, hiring the best
Greek and foreign artists and architects to design the convent buildings, and execute the intricate wood carvings and
frescoes, icons and shrines. The convent was designed to be
independent of the town of Oinoussai, having its own farm-
lands, harbor, and helicopter landing strip. Every modern
convenience was installed including private bathrooms for
each nun. Inside the walls, in addition to the living quarters,
there was a small church and a separate mausoleum to
house the bones of Mrs. Pateras's family.

After three years, as is the custom throughout Greece,
Irene's body was exhumed in order to put her bones in the
family mausoleum. But when her corpse was uncovered it
had not disintegrated but mummified. The body was intact
except for one finger that was inadvertently broken off by
the men who were digging up the grave. When a body is
exhumed in a state of preservation, it is considered by many
Greeks to be a sign of sainthood. Mrs. Pateras was convinced that her daughter was a saint, and removed the
corpse to the convent in Oinoussai. The Metropolitan of
Chios ruled that the body must be reburied until the flesh
decayed. "To keep a body unburied is both unholy and
illegal," he said, but Mrs. Pateras refused to yield. Irene's
body can now be viewed in a glass-topped coffin in the
mausoleum.

The convent, of which Mrs. Pateras is now the abbess,

is run according to the strictest rules and only women may enter its doors. The fifteen or so nuns who live inside come from all over, including one American woman and one Canadian. There is little information given out about the occupants—perhaps as a result of widespread publicity in the early sixties when the family of the American nun, Christine Coryell, claimed that she had been spirited away to the convent and was being held against her will. A diplomatic incident threatened until her family went to Oinoussai and faced the nun, who told them she was there at her own choice.

To get to the convent of Evangelismos it is necessary to have the local priest of Oinoussai drive you there. After a journey of about twenty minutes over precipitous mountain roads, my wife and I and the priest arrived and knocked at the ornate main doors. A small panel in one door was opened and a nun looked out. Speaking in Greek, I obtained permission for my wife to enter. After her hair was covered with a scarf, she was led on a tour of the convent by a young woman, evidently a novice, who spoke only Greek and declined to say how many women were housed there. The tour did not include the living quarters, and my wife only glimpsed one nun. She noticed that the offerings attached to the icons of the saints in the church, instead of the usual hammered metal votive figures, were expensive wristwatches and pieces of jewelry. When she was led into the mausoleum she found the body of Irene, in her glass coffin, draped entirely in black except for the hands. One hand was exposed to show the mummified state of her corpse, the other hand was encased in a solid silver glove. When my wife turned around, she was startled to find another corpse on display: the remains of Panagos Pateras himself, who died not long after his daughter was exhumed, when his cancer recurred. Near the end he too took orders, became a monk, and was given a monk's burial. When his bones were exhumed, they were gathered together, including his false teeth, and put in a glass-fronted case on one side of the mausoleum door. An empty case on the other side of the door awaits the remains of his wife, the abbess.

The existence of the convent of Evangelismos is a source of controversy among the shipowners of Oinoussai. They are all devout members of the Greek Orthodox Church, and they hesitate to criticize the widow Pateras for her efforts on behalf of the convent and her daughter's memory. On the other hand, using her husband's fortune for a multimillion-dollar convent makes them uneasy. Most Greek shipowners want their ships and their fortunes passed on after their death to their children, a chain of succession that is the very foundation of Oinoussai's economy. Therefore, Mrs. Pateras's departure from tradition disturbs even her late husband's family. One of her close relatives remarked to me with some irony, "I've heard of taking gold out of a mountain, but this is the first time I've ever seen gold poured back into a mountain."

Although the Pateras and Lemos clans are the most numerous and wealthiest of the great Oinoussian shipping families, there are several others who command numerous ships. Their names are Lyras, Lignos, Samonas, Pontikos, and Mavrophilipas, among others.

The half dozen Oinoussians who make their homes in New York—including Nicholas Lyras, Nicholas Lygnos, and Nicholas Pateras—maintain close ties to each other and never lose touch with their *patrida*. They receive the newspaper from Oinoussai, and most of them manage to get back to the island frequently.

The choice of the right husband or wife, difficult enough in any society, is greatly complicated in Oinoussai, especially when the union of great shipping fortunes is involved.

There is a well-defined circle of acceptance for an Oinoussian choosing a mate, and even those living abroad adhere to it. Most desirable, of course, is a wife from one of the other Oinoussian shipping clans. Next best is a shipping Greek from Chios, the nearest major island to Oinoussai. Still acceptable is a member of a Greek shipping dynasty from some other island. A Greek who is neither from Oinoussai nor in shipping is considered a controversial choice, and if a son or daughter of a shipping family selects a non-Greek, it can produce dramatic repercussions. One young man, who had long lived in London but was the scion of an Oinoussian shipping family, decided to marry an English model. They invited the London shipping Greeks to their wedding in Saint Sophia Cathedral, but on the wedding day no one showed up. As the bride and groom waited at the door of the church, a large limousine pulled up. The mother of the groom, who had come all the way from Oinoussai, got out and walked resolutely up the steps of the church. While the bride and the priest stared, she slapped her son hard across the face, then turned and stormed back to the waiting car. The bride never was accepted within the circle of London Oinoussians.

"Oinoussai" in Greek means "the wine islands." Oinoussai is actually a cluster of nine tiny islands, but only the largest is inhabited. It has been settled since ancient times and was mentioned in the writings of Herodotus, Thucydides, and Saint Luke. During the Middle Ages, the inhabitants abandoned the island because it was so vulnerable to pirate raids, and in the early part of the eighteenth century a few settlers made their way back to the island—shepherds from the town of Kardamila on the nearby island of Chios, looking for grazing land for their flocks. The residents of Kardamila are considered the toughest inhabitants of Chios, and those who were enterprising enough to resettle Oinoussai were considered the hardiest of the lot. They clung to the island, living as shepherds and vintners, for a hundred years. During the War of Independence, when most of the population of Chios was massacred by the Turks, the Oinoussians fled to the island of Syros, which was then the major shipping center of the Aegean. "There they opened their eyes," wrote Andreas Lemos, the historian of Oinoussai. When the Oinoussians were able to return to their island five years after a Turkish amnesty they "threw themselves in a body into shipping," according to Lemos. Their qualities of toughness, enterprise, and group loyalty fitted them perfectly for the sea. They began by buying small ships in order to trade in the Aegean and during the Crimean War did a booming business carrying supplies for Turkey from Smyrna to Constantinople. They amassed capital and bought bigger ships. By 1868, they had thirty ships ranging from 40 to 160 tons. This allowed them to extend their frontiers beyond the Aegean to the Black, Adriatic, and the Mediterranean Seas.

In 1905, three Oinoussians—a Hadjipateras, a Pateras, and a Lemos—formed a partnership to buy the island's first steam-powered ship. With it they entered the Atlantic market. At the outbreak of World War II, Oinoussians had accumulated sixty-five steamships weighing from 2,000 to 9,000 tons each. The Oinoussian fleet was all but destroyed in the war. Only seven ships survived and nearly every family on the island mourned a son or husband who had gone down with his ship. After the war, the United States put on the market surplus Liberty ships and allocated one hundred ships to the Greek government. Permisson to buy these ships was given out on the basis of how many each shipowner had lost. With the fourteen Liberty ships they were allowed to buy, the Oinoussians began again to rebuild— succeeding so well that the tonnage they now own exceeds the size of the navies of many countries.

With every turn of the economy, with every opening or closing of the Suez Canal, or post-war recession, dozens of shipowners—Greek and non-Greek—have gone under. How have the Oinoussians managed to ride every economic wave without being caught in the undercurrents? Every Oinoussian has an answer. No doubt each one is partly correct. "We succeed," said Captain Nicholas Lygnos, who now directs a ship management firm in New York, "because we follow the rules of our fathers—work hard, save every penny, and take good care of your ships." Captain Lygnos went to sea at sixteen but was immersed in shipping long before that. "When you're an Oinoussian, from the time you're born, all you hear is ships," he says. "Even here in New York, that's all we talk about at my house."

Oinoussians are known for being conservative with their money. They always keep ample cash in reserve so that they can take advantage of promising developments or rebuild when disaster befalls them. They are also notoriously competitive. "In the last century," said Captain Theodoros Lemos, "we competed against shipowners from Galaxidi who then dominated the Eastern Mediterranean. Now they're gone and we're competing against shipowners from all over the world." Costa Lemos is often quoted as saying, "I will help anyone except a competitor."

Oinoussians will compete fiercely against each other— even brother against brother—but when there is an outside danger, they quickly draw together for mutual protection. In the nineteenth century, because they could not get insurance on their ships, a single sinking often would wipe out a family. The Oinoussians banded together to form their own insurance company. Today every Oinoussian is keenly aware of his duty to his "compatriots" from the same island. "When the knife reaches the bone," says Nicholas Lyras, who also manages ships in New York, "we'll help each other. We don't want one of our own to fail." Of the many theories as to why Oinoussians succeed at shipping above all other Greeks, perhaps the best explanation was given by Konstantine Hadjipateras, founder of the Hadji-pateras clan, who died in 1943 at the age of eighty-seven. In his memoirs he wrote,

> Without wishing to boast, I attribute our progress to certain moral qualities: our energetic applicaton, our efficiency, our thrift, the austerity of our family life in Oinoussai and, let me add, our inborn flair for business. Our progress seems all the more remarkable for our obscurity. We were quite unknown to the outside world, quite without protection and had neither capital nor education. That is why we feel proud of ourselves.

FOURTEEN

Going Home

"Of all peoples, the Greeks have dreamt
the dream of life best."
GOETHE

When arriving in Greece, whether by plane or ship, train or automobile, there is always a feeling of going home, although it may be a first visit. "In one way or another, at some time or other, we have all been there, even if only in a dream," wrote Henry Miller, whose eight-month visit to the country shortly before World War II became a series of life-enhancing experiences for him and produced *The Colossus of Maroussi*, one of the most popular books about traveling in Greece ever written.

It is not the familiarity of the Greek landscape that creates the immediate bond one feels with Greece on arrival. In fact, the landscape is quite different from any found in the United States, Northern Europe, or even the Western Mediterranean. As Lord Kinross noted, "In the west, Europe flowers; in the east, it is laid bare. The landscape of Italy smiles, all soft and caressing; that of Greece stares, challenging and tough. Here in the eastern Mediterranean is the hard core of Europe, a land reduced to its essentials of light and form, of rock and sky and sea." But it is the interplay of these essentials that grabs the attention, ex-

235

pands the imagination, and revives the spirit. To watch the landscape of Greece, stark and unfamiliar as it may be, is to experience a rare sense of fulfillment and serenity. "Nothing is lacking in Greece; it lies before us, a complete, firmly delineated world, a self-contained microcosm which includes every basic element of the earth, and all within our range of vision," wrote Ioannis Gaitanides. "Plain and mountain are not separated, they are always together, each enhancing the effect of the other, like a picture and its frame; the plain, the contents of the vessel, fills it up, but the mountains enclose, delimit, hold it together; their crests run in a long horizontal, seldom broken by a peak. At last they come to an end, and there is no vertical line to tempt our eyes upward. But the sea drives deep furrows far into the land, which seems to be stretching out its legs, drawing the waves into its lap . . ."

Scattered about the landscape of Greece are the monuments of its history—the oracles, the temples, the fortresses, the churches. Greece is beautiful and varied enough to offer visitors a memorable journey without seeing a single ruin, but that would be unfortunate. Nothing explains contemporary Greece nor dramatizes our ties to it more than a visit to an ancient monument in its own setting. Touching the pieces of a shattered pillar, looking at a row of broken columns on a hillside, the mind seeks to restore what once was, and in that vision we glimpse how much of what we build, dream, create, believe, and value is Greek.

The birthplace of Western thought and culture is found in Athens in and around the Acropolis. Mankind realized a magnificent moment in its history there, and returning to it is like reliving the happiest time of one's youth. Architecture and sculpture reached a peak that has never been equaled, and enough of it is still left on the Acropolis to thrill and inspire every visitor. On a slope below the Parthenon is the Theater of Dionysus where the tragedies of Aeschylus, Sophocles, and Euripides were first performed. With the exception of Shakespeare, no dramatist has every approached, let alone equaled, their power. And on a nearby hill, democracy was born and flourished. Mankind had learned much earlier that a society could not prosper without order, but until the Greeks it was believed that order could only be achieved through despotism. The East could never conceive of order in any other way and all great civilizations before Greece were a succession of tyrannies. The West discovered a way to achieve order through freedom in Greece.

The Greek contribution to the Western heritage did not end with the Golden Age of Pericles. Philosophers such as Socrates, Plato, and Aristotle as well as historians such as Herodotus and Thucydides taught mankind that the worst dangers it faced were passion and ignorance. Men could remain free if they were willing to control their own freedom. The lesson was not lost on the founders of the United States, who shaped its constitution on the Athenian model but injected checks and balances to avoid the kind of excesses that destroyed Athenian democracy. "In all very numerous assemblies, passion never fails to wrest the sceptre from reason," James Madison wrote. "Had every Athenian citizen been a Socrates, every Athenian assembly would still have been a mob."

The contributions of Greeks to Western civilization continued for a thousand years after Athens became a backwater of the Roman empire, through the works of such men as Euclid, Archimedes, Meleager, Galen, Zeno, Epictetus, and Plutarch.

Christianity was spread throughout the Mediterranean world in Greek as Saint Paul preached and wrote in the language, and the Gospels, with the possible exception of Matthew, were first written down in Greek. When power in the Roman empire shifted to Byzantium, its administration remained Roman but its language and culture became Greek. For the next millenium, Hellenic influence in art and architecture was profound, as a visit to any monastery or Byzantine church demonstrates. After the fall of Constantinople in 1453, thousands of Byzantine scholars fled to Italy and became a catalyst for the Renaissance, which was fueled by a passion for Hellenic art, literature, and philosophy.

As the Renaissance spread to northern Europe, Greek legends, images, and ideals captured the imagination of a succession of writers, artists, and thinkers including Chaucer, Rabelais, Shakespeare, Milton, John Locke, Goethe, Titian, Byron, Wordsworth, Delacroix, Keats, Shelley, Thomas Jefferson, Yeats, Joyce, Anouilh, and Tolstoy, who began teaching himself Greek at forty-two. "Without a knowledge of Greek, there is no education," he determined.

The immense Greek contribution to Western civilization is both a source of pride and a kind of burden to the people living in Greece today, as is expressed in the poem by Nobel laureate George Seferis:

> I woke with this marble head in my hands;
> it exhausts my elbows and I don't know where to put
>   it down

Whatever insecurities Greeks may feel about their past, they insist that they are the progeny of Pericles and Plato even though they may look more like Aristotle Onassis than the Hermes of Praxiteles. Although there may not be many wide-browed, straight-nosed, light-complexioned Greeks walking around Athens or Corinth today, their claim is not without foundation. "As in all Western countries, the disruption caused by successive invasions has made the idea of race obsolete in Greece, but it has left intact the much richer conception of a people," French writers Jeanne and George Roux observed. "More than a race, more than a nation, the Greeks are a people. The face of the people changes because the face is alive. Without ever being exactly the same, it is never entirely different and the alterations introduced by history never eliminate the permanent fundamentals."

What are these fundamentals? One is a strong feeling of equality inherited directly from their ancestors. "Differences of situation or fortune never prevent a Greek from feeling himself the equal as a human being of any other man, whoever he may be," wrote Mr. and Mrs. Roux. "Success and wealth are considered the result of *savoir faire*; they signify intelligence, astuteness or luck and the rich would no more dream of concealing their richness than the poor of being annoyed by it even if they envy it. A Greek peasant is perfectly at ease with a minister; a minister is not self-conscious with a peasant. They are two similar men placed differently by destiny."

The scholar Edith Hamilton, comparing previous civilizatons to the Greek, noted that earlier cultures were preoccupied with death and focused all their art on it, while Greeks turned full face to life. "To rejoice in life, to find the world beautiful and delightful to live in, was a mark of the Greek spirit which distinguished it from all that had gone before," she wrote. The joy of life is as evident in Greeks today as it was in their ancestors. "Children still of their light and landscape, close to the earth that bore them and to the seas that carried them to wider horizons, they are a people forever wide awake to life in all its aspects," observed Lord Kinross.

Because of the people, the rhythm of life seems to beat stronger and quicker in Greece than anywhere else. It is felt as soon as you leave the plane at an airport or disembark at a dock and watch passengers greeting relatives and friends who have come to meet them. The jostling, the shouting, the weeping and embracing are familiar from other airports and other harbors, but they are more intense in Greece than in New York and London or even Lisbon and Naples. The strong beat of life is felt in the waterfront tavernas and village squares as Greeks gather to talk, drink, sing, dance, and argue about everything from politics to the price of olives. It is felt in the streets, the sidewalk cafés, the balconies, the shops, the homes, and the schoolyards. It is evident even in church, where worshipers don't sit silently in pews but stand in knots in the unfurnished nave, chanting, whispering, shifting restlessly, and sending an antiphony of sounds floating throughout the edifice along with the incense.

Greeks disdain quiet and solitude. They find little joy in going out for a walk alone or scant pleasure in having dinner with one companion. Their happiness is not complete unless they can enjoy it surrounded by a *parea*, or a group of friends. They move about their cities and towns in these *pareas* laughing, shouting, teasing each other, and always ready to add to the company congenial acquaintances and even strangers encountered along the way. Being with a good *parea* in Greece is like going to a picnic, having a birthday party, and joining a family reunion all at the same time. Greeks are perhaps the most gregarious people in the world, and they find it easy to strike up conversations because they are not constrained by superfluous etiquette. But while they may be joyful and generous acquaintances, they can be demanding and even difficult friends. They are adamant in their positions no matter how shaky, unwilling to grant any merit to an opposing view and easy to anger. "Their life is a struggle against truth; they are vicious in their own defense," Lord Byron concluded after several months in Greece, although he found their attributes worthy enough to give up his life to help the Greeks win their independence from the Turks.

"A thousand faces has this Greek world, some of them cruel, mad, horrible too, but the abiding, authentic features always recognizable," wrote Henry Miller. "The male Greek today, for example, despite all the variations of type, despite the fact that he no longer has the blood of the gods in him, comes closer to our conception of Western man than any other in Europe. His manhood reveals itself in the curious fusion of weakness and strength. He is just as curious, just as garrulous, just as susceptible as the Greek of old. He still weeps openly and unashamedly, like the heroes of Homer."

While Greeks today have much in common with their noble ancestors, there is much in which they differ as well. The quality that the ancient Greeks valued most, and which is rather scarce today, is *sophrosune*, a word best translated as self-control but embodying the spirit behind the great Delphic sayings, "Know Thyself" and "Nothing in Excess." As Edith Hamilton wrote,

> Arrogance, insolent self assertion, was of all qualities most detested by the Greeks. *Sophrosune* was the exact opposite. . . . It meant accepting the bounds of excellence laid down by human nature, restraining impulses of unrestricted freedom, shunning excess, obeying the inner laws of harmony and proportion. This was the virtue Greeks esteemed above all others, not because they were moderate lovers of the golden mean, but because their spontaneity and ever-changing variety and ardent energy of life had to have the strong

control of a disciplined spirit or end in senseless violence.

When the Greeks achieved a high degree of *sophrosune*, they defeated the Persians and created the Parthenon. But when they started losing it through arrogance and greed, they fell on each other until they became so weak that first the Macedonians and then the Romans took away their freedom.

But the ideal was not destroyed. It lives on not only for the Greeks who occupy the land where it flourished, but for everyone who believes in it and goes there to nourish the dream. For all those who love the light of reason and the joy of life, who strive for the best in themselves, and who value truth and freedom, Greece is home.

INDEX

ABOUT THE AUTHOR

Nicholas Gage, who was born Nicholas Gatzoyiannis in Greece in 1939, is the author of three books and a former investigative reporter and foreign correspondent for *The New York Times*. A graduate of Boston University and the Columbia University Graduate School of Journalism, Mr. Gage's work as an investigative reporter won numerous journalistic honors and was collected in two books. He is also the author of two novels, *Bones of Contention* and *The Bourlotas Fortune,* a dynastic saga about Greek shipowners.

In 1977 he was assigned as the *Times* regional correspondent in Athens, and covered political and revolutionary upheavals throughout the Middle East for the next four years. In 1981 he left the paper to write *Eleni*, about his family's struggle to survive the waves of war and revolution that engulfed Greece in the 1940s.

Published by Random House to wide critical acclaim, *Eleni* was a main selection of the Book-of-the-Month Club, won the Heinemann Prize as the best book of the year from the Royal Society of Literature of Great Britain, and has been translated into fourteen languages. A movie version was released in 1985 by Warner Bros.

Mr. Gage lives in Grafton, Massachusetts, with his wife, Joan, and three children, Christos, Eleni, and Marina.